How To W Home And Be A Full Time Online Reseller Box Set

Learn How To Make A Living Buying From Thrift Stores And Reselling On eBay

Included Books

Turning Thrift Store Vintage Toys Into Stacks Of Cash

Turning Thrift Store Oddities And Rarities Into Cool Cash

Turning Thrift Store Electronics And Gadgets Into Cash Magic

Thrifting And Winning

Reseller Secrets To Dominating A Thrift Store Revealed

Selling Creative DIY Projects Online

Table of Contents

Book 1: Turning Thrift Store Vintage Toys Into Stacks Of Cash

Chapter 7: Knowing What to Look for

Conclusion

Book 2: Turning Thrift Store Oddities And Rarities Into Cool Cash

Book 3: Turning Thrift Store Electronics And Gadgets Into Cash Magic

Book 4: Thrifting And Winning

Book 5: Reseller Secrets To Dominating A Thrift Store Revealed

Book 6: Selling Creative DIY Projects Online

TURNING THRIFT STORE VINTAGE TOYS INTO STACKS OF CASH

50 VINTAGE AND COLLECTIBLE TOYS YOU CAN BUY CHEAP AT THRIFT STORES AND RESELL ON EBAY AND AMAZON FOR HUGE PROFIT

RICK RILEY

Introduction

I want to thank you for downloading the book, *Turning Thrift Store Vintage Toys into Stacks of Cash: 50 Vintage and Collectible Toys You Can Buy Cheap at Thrift Stores and Resell On eBay And Amazon for Huge Profit.*

This book contains proven steps and strategies on how to find vintage toys in your local thrift store that will sell for a good amount of cash when resold online. Most of us don't know what toys will be worth money when we walk past them in a thrift store. To us, they seem like some child's used toys that need to be loved. However, there are massive treasures to be found if you are willing to look past the surface.

Finding vintage toys in a thrift store can be a quick and easy way to make some extra money. Collectors are forever looking for old toys to add to their collections, and they are willing to pay mad money for them. Why not take advantage of this opportunity? In this book, I'm going to provide you with some of the vintage toys that you can find in a thrift store that collectors will pay top dollar for. Why not give it a try?

Thanks again for downloading this book, I hope you enjoy it!

Chapter 1- Dolls and Other Girls' Toys

In the wonderful world of thrift store shopping, there is a wide array of choices for everyone to look for. Some are simply old toys that a parent forced the child to part with because they had outgrown it. Others came from attics where they had sat for years, waiting for children to come and play with them. However their lives had started, they had all ended up in one common place: your local thrift store.

While some people don't think twice about getting rid of used toys and games, others have a sentimental link to them that makes it difficult for them to part with them. People may have had such a toy in their past that they would like to find once more. A lot of toys are only made for a limited time, so it can be difficult to find the same toy five to ten years after you have parted ways with it. However, if they existed once, they will be found again.

Many people turn to the internet to find such toys. How do you know which toys are being sought out? You can either turn to the internet or take a look at the timeless vintage toys that always seem to be in style. In this chapter, I'm going to list some of the girls' toys and dolls that make big money online.

Barbie Dolls

As time has gone on, Barbie dolls have become made of less expensive materials. So, if you can find the dolls that are mad out of heavy plastic, then you're looking at a collectable.

However, knowing your Barbies and the year that they were released will also help you to find rare and collectable dolls that people will pay good money for.

Old Plastic Dolls

Just like Barbie dolls, older dolls were made out of different materials. Heavy plastic, porcelain dolls, and those made of celluloid are all collectible and valuable for you to purchase. You can definitely tell an older doll by its materials and facial characteristics. They most often won't have moveable eyes or ones that are weighted. Also, they don't tend to be equipped to make much noise. There are older dolls that do boast these characteristics, but for the most part, they are plain and made of older materials.

Troll Dolls

Remember those crazy-haired dolls that promised good luck if you rubbed their tummies? Well, they are now a collector's items. Keep your eyes peeled for these goofy looking dolls while you scour your local thrift stores.

Old Tea Sets

Every little girl had a tea set. Well, now the older the tea set, the more valuable it is. Also, tea sets from overseas and made of porcelain are worth money. Also, be watchful of tea sets boasting characters from television shows or Disney movies. These are great ways to make a few extra bucks.

Kewpie Dolls

These adorable little dolls with the plastic curl on top of their heads have because a collector's item within the past ten years. You can find them in antique stores, but you might stand a good chance at finding some in thrift stores as well. The better condition that they're in, the more money they are worth.

Raggedy Ann and Andy Dolls

Again, these are common around antique stores, but they are also valuable when resold online. When looking through the toys, try to find authentic Raggedy Ann and Andy dolls in their original clothing. Collectors will pay top dollar for authentic dolls in good shape with original clothing.

Little Orphan Annie Toys and Outfits

Little Orphan Annie was a popular toy line in the early 1980s. Today, the dolls and the different accessories and clothing for the dolls are coveted by collectors. However, make sure that the clothing and dolls are authentic prior to purchasing them.

Rainbow Brite Dolls

Rainbow Brite and all of her friends were popular with the little girls in the 1980s. It's more difficult to find these dolls anymore, so if you see one, you know it will be a good investment!

Strawberry Shortcake Dolls

Strawberry Shortcake and the dolls that are a part of her clan are sought after by collectors. Be careful when buying these. You want to make sure that they are authentic and that the dolls themselves are in decent shape. Since collectors look at items that are in good shape, this is a good rule of thumb whenever you are looking at vintage toys.

Cabbage Patch Dolls

The original Cabbage Patch Dolls are one of the top items that people look for when searching for vintage dolls. The thing with the Cabbage Patch kid dolls, however, is that there was a knockoff of these that were sold in craft stores for crafting purposes. So, be aware of the characteristics of a real Cabbage Patch doll when observing these on a thrift store shelf.

While these are only a few of the toys that you might be able to resell for money on eBay, know that a lot of older toys to show wear and tear and other such damage. Take this into account when searching for toys. Some of these defects can be easily overcome, but others are beyond repair. I will cover what to look for in the way of damages in a later chapter.

Out of girls' toys, dolls are the most popular to be resold as a vintage toy. The other great thing about this is that thrift stores often have tons of dolls for you to look through. When looking through the selection, keep your eyes peeled for certain brands of dolls and the age of the dolls. These are both good indicators of whether or not they are considered vintage.

Chapter 2- Flashback to Your Childhood

It might make you feel old, but many of the toys that were popular during your childhood have come back with resounding popularity. Not only do collectors seek these out, but will also pay high prices to get their hands on some of these toys. With vintage toys, it's important that they are in good repair with as little damage as possible. If the buyer will have to restore it, then you will not get the highest price out of the sale. Keep this in mind as you're looking for vintage toys in your local thrift store. Even if you're not too old, toys from your childhood might still be considered vintage. It all depends on when they were made and their popularity when they were originally sold. In this chapter, I'm going to list some of the vintage toys that might just make you flashback to your own childhood!

Vintage Teenage Mutant Ninja Turtle Figurines

With the recent comeback of the children's cartoon, Teenage Mutant Ninja Turtles, the old figurines and toys associated with the original series are in high demand amongst toy enthusiasts and collectors. The toy line came out with many different toys and figurines during the original show's popularity in the early 1990s. So, look for these older toys when looking through thrift store shelves.

Beanie Babies

The original Beanie Babies have been a highly collectable item for some time now. Beanie Babies will have tags on them stating the animal's name and birthdate. People like to find Beanie Babies that have birthdates that coincide with their own. You might have heard some rumors about the original toys. They still have a high popularity rate, even with the viral internet scare of them being stuffed with spiders' eggs. Don't worry, they are perfectly safe, and people who collect them are looking for specific ones to complete their collection.

Pogs

The game of Pogs was played amongst preteens and teens during the 1990s. The challenge of turning these cardboard circles over with a metal disc happened to appeal to children. They were often found in abundance, but now they are a collectable item. So, if you should come across the cardboards circles and metal discs, know that they can be resold for cash!

Trading Card Games

There are a lot of trading card games that were popular throughout the 1990s that are still popular today. These card games have come out with different series based upon the year. The older cards that are not being made anymore, or those that are rare, are worth money to collectors. Look for card games such as Pokémon, Magic, My Little Pony, and Yu Gi Oh. These stand the highest chance of having collectable and coveted cards!

Lincoln Logs

These connectable logs were used to build houses and other such structures. They consisted of log looking pieces that had grooves at the ends, making them stackable. When put together, they had the feel of a log cabin. Since these are not made the way they used to be made, the original Lincoln Logs are worth some money when resold online.

Old Legos

Legos are a type of toy that is still highly popular today. However, when they first came out, they weren't as complex and specialized as they are today. The original Legos came in smaller sets and gradually evolved into the huge sets we see today. If you can find a complete set of old Legos, you can stand the chance of making some major cash when you resell them online.

Vintage Stuffed Animals

Most people can tell when a stuffed animal is old. They tend to lack tags and other markers that they were mass made. Older stuffed animals are also made of different materials. So, when looking at stuffed animals, take into account the material that they are made of and whether or not they have tags. These are good indicators of whether or not they are vintage.

Cast Iron Toys

Since the new movement towards toy safety, toys are no longer made out of cast iron. The heavy material could hurt children if the toys are not played with appropriately. So, if you find toys made of cast iron, it's a good indicator that they are vintage. There are a wide array of cast iron toys that can be searched for, ranging from toy vehicles to doll house furniture.

Fisher Price Toys before 1975

Fisher Price, a company that is known for creating toys for young children, is a highly sought out brand when looking at vintage toys. The older toys from this company are collected by toy enthusiasts. A good indicator of whether they are considered vintage is when they were made. As a general rule, I like to place the toys before 1975 into the category of vintage.

Mr. Potato Head

Mr. Potato Head and his family have long been a favorite amongst children. Who else will let you change their facial appearances on a daily basis? The older models of these toys and their accessories are a popular purchase online. So, the next time you find yourself face to face with a Mr. Potato Head doll, think twice before passing him by!

Disney Character Items

Since the Disney cartoons have touched many generations, toys based upon the characters found in their movies and cartoons are highly coveted by collectors. The older the toys, the more that they will be worth. You can easily tell which of these toys are older based upon the details of the toy. The older Mickey Mouse characters have larger features. So, by knowing which of these toys are older, you stand a better chance at finding a vintage Disney toy.

If you see a toy that reminds you of your childhood, depending on your age, chances are that it is no longer made and that it can be worth some serious cash. Take some time and look through the selection of toys in your thrift store, and if you have any doubts about the age of the toy, pick it up. Go with your gut instinct. The worst that can happen is that you're out a few bucks and end up re-donating a toy!

Chapter 3- Boys' Toys and Other Fun

Just like toys that were made to cater to little girls, there is a large amount of toys that are for boys that are now worth money. The selection of these toys is a little more diverse for boys, so you stand a better chance at finding something vintage for a boy. However, a lot of toys were never gender specific, so they can fall into any category. In this chapter, I'm going cover the main toys that are high in popularity that were made for boys.

Soldier Figurines

If you think about little boys, one of the toys that are commonly associated with them are soldiers. Soldier dolls and figurines are highly collectable and popular. Depending on the type of material that they are made of, these can bring in varying amounts of cash.

Hot Wheels Cars

Hot Wheels cars, especially the ones that are no longer made, are sought out by collectors. In their time, Hot Wheels have come out with many limited edition toys that collectors would love to get their hands on. While looking through toys, take note of the year that the car or truck was made. It's often printed on the bottom of the car with the Hot Wheels logo. Like other popular toys, Hot Wheels has a lot of knock offs that look similar, but are not worth anything.

Metal Dump Trucks

The old heavy metal dump trucks that little boys used to have are now a vintage toy item. The companies have stopped making these out of metal due to the dangers that sharp edges may cause children. Even though they have stopped making these toys, people will seek out the old metal dump trucks because they are durable and will last for a long time.

Star Wars Figurines and Accessories

Star Wars has been a long time favorite for many generations. With that being said, it stands to reason that the toys and figurines that come from the movie are collectible items. The older the item, the greater the possibility of it being worth some major cash. So, keep yourself on the lookout for Star Wars items!

Super Hero Toys and Accessories

The super heroes from the comic books have been a favorite to adults and children alike. From Superman to the Hulk, items that boast super hero logos and likenesses are popular and will sell for big money. I know that Batman and Superman were popular during my own childhood and are still popular with children today. Use the knowledge of super heroes to find items that you will be able to make a huge profit off of.

Ventriloquist Dolls

Ventriloquist dolls were an extremely popular toy among young boys in the sixties and seventies. The ability to have a doll that you could make talk was very appealing. Even though they are not popular with the children today, these dolls are still collected.

GI Joe Dolls and Accessories

GI Joe was a role model for young boys around the time of the Vietnam War. Having this fictional role model helped boys achieve creativity and bravery. The dolls and accessories remained popular for many years, and now the toys are being sold for nice profits.

Transformers

Based upon a cartoon, these vehicles that turn into action figures were a favorite among young boys. By moving their parts around, you could either have a vehicle or a person. These characters would fight the bad guys and win. The show no longer exists, but the toys can still be found and resold for stacks of cash.

Erector Sets

Erector sets were a project where a child could build structures using metal parts. This toy catered to older boys, and it was challenging and fun for them. They were only marketed for a short time, but people still seek to collect them.

Toys gain popularity for various reasons. By knowing what children enjoyed during the past, you will have a good idea of what will be collected now. Also, look at what's popular now. Trends tend to repeat themselves, so toys that were popular during your childhood may become popular once more. Take this into account when shopping in your local thrift store.

Chapter 4- Games and Puzzles

Every child likes games and puzzles. As they have evolved with time, the older versions of some games have faded into the past, while others remain strong up to this day. Depending on how rare and popular the games were, you can stand a chance at making a good profit by finding and reselling vintage games and puzzles. It might be difficult to figure out whether or not these items are considered vintage, but they tend to follow some of the same rules as the other toys in this book do.

In this chapter, I'm going to highlight some of the main toys and puzzles that are searched for and bought frequently online.

Old Wooden Blocks

The old fashioned wooden blocks that young children used to use to learn their letters and numbers are considered a vintage item that can be worth some money, depending on how old they are. When looking at wooden blocks that have the alphabet and numbers painted on them, take a look at the quality of the wood and that will help you determine the age of the block. The older blocks tend to be made out of high quality wood.

Pinball Machines

Whether it be a tabletop machine or a full pinball machine like you would find in an arcade, collectors are looking for these to add to their collections. Since arcades are becoming less popular, these machines have started to fade into the background, making them a good item to resell when found.

Table Hockey

Table hockey or air hockey tables are another type of collectible game that will resell very well online. As with pinball machines, since arcades are becoming less popular, these have faded out with time. Having a good and quality table will certainly earn you some nice cash.

Chess Sets

Chess is a highly popular game all over the world. With that said, there are multiple variations of chess sets. I have seen them range from cartoon characters to intricate figurines that grace an ornate board. Since there are so many variations of pieces, people will buy ones that suit their fancy. Older sets are collected as antiques and people will pay a good amount of money to buy a set that suits them.

Cribbage Boards

Cribbage is a classic game that involves moving your pieces around a small but intricate board. These boards have been in circulation for many years, so the older the board, the more money you can fetch when selling it online. A lot of cribbage boards are made out of wood, so follow the hints in looking at the quality of the wood. The pieces are often stored in a slot underneath the board, so if it has a metal door, you know it is of higher quality than those that are made with plastic.

Original Board Games

Vintage board games have a nice level of popularity online. Take Monopoly for example. The original game came out in the 1930s and several variations of the game have come along since then. Having an old Monopoly game can earn you a nice chunk of change if all of the pieces are present and the board is in good shape. There are other original board games that can be considered vintage, so think back to what games were popular during your childhood and see if you can resell them online if you should happen upon them in a thrift store.

Maj Jong Tiles

Nowadays, one can play Maj Jong on the computer. However, the game originated centuries ago, using brightly colored tiles that you set up and tried to match in order to complete the puzzle. These tiles are worth some good money if you can find a unique or intricate set.

Wooden Puzzles

You probably remember the heavy wooden puzzles that young children played with before they graduated to the more detailed puzzles. Some of these puzzles are very old and worth a lot of money. Depending on the condition of the puzzle and whether or not all of the pieces are present are also other factors that will determine the profitability of these when resold online.

Finding a game or puzzle that can be resold online basically depends on the factors of having all of the pieces of the game and the condition of the game itself. Knowing this, try and find games and puzzles that have all or most of their components. You will be better able to resell these online. If a game is missing pieces, then it is difficult to find them anywhere if the game is out of production. Think like a collector when looking at these items. This will help you determine if it is a worthwhile purchase or a waste of time and money.

Chapter 5- Other Toys that Can be Worth Money

After covering the basic categories of toys, I realized that there are still some toys that really don't fit into the other categories, but they still can be considered vintage toys and worth some money when resold. So, I thought that I would devote this chapter to these toys that don't really fit inside the definitions of the other categories. As mentioned before, this is not an extensive list, but it is a list of the most popular toys to be bought online.

Pull and Push Toys

Wooden pull and push toys that were popular for young children are a hot item to be resold online. These toys typically made motions while the child would pull it or push it along, making it seem as though the child were leading an animal on a leash. These might seem simple at face value, but they are considered vintage and collectors will pay good money for these toys in good condition. The best quality and most likely to resell are going to be the wooden toys that still work properly.

My Little Pony

My Little Pony dolls and trading cards fit into the category because they are not necessarily popular with little girls. Grown men have taken a fancy to the card game and collecting the dolls. By finding the toys and the cards, you are basically guaranteeing yourself a sell online. Be careful about fakes though. There are pony figurines that will closely resemble the My Little Pony horses, but they are not the originals. So, when you come across an older looking My Little Pony horse, don't discount it as some poor reject from a little girl's collection.

Pez Machines

Pez machines might not seem like a toy, but kids love to play with them. Another thing about Pez machines is that there are millions of different ones and new ones are becoming available regularly. Since when a new machine is released there is only limited availability, collectors are willing to pay more if they cannot find the toy in stores or anywhere else. The older Pez machines are also highly collectable because they are no longer in production and coming across them is rare.

Waterfuls

These water games made for hours of entertainment for young children. The point of the game was to use water pressure to accomplish tasks such as placing rings around poles and moving small balls around a watery game land. These were popular in the 1990s, and finding one in good condition will definitely interest an avid collector.

Cap Guns

Cap guns were a realistic version of a real gun that even made a similar sound. You would put in cartridges that would pop when you pulled the trigger on the gun. Boys and girls alike liked to play cops and robbers using these realistic guns.

Yo-yos

Yo-yos are another type of toy that has evolved over time. They started out as wooded discs on a rope that would return when thrown correctly. As time went on, the wood was replaced by plastic and other variations of materials. These are a great selling item if you can find the old wooden yo-yos or one of the older plastic yo-yos.

View Masters

View Masters were a toy where a child could put in a disc and view whatever the discs had printed on them. It was kind of like looking a picture's negative with a magnifying glass. When you would hit the trigger, the disc would turn and a new picture or scene would fill your line of vision. There were multiple types of discs that could be viewed in these toys, ranging from scenery to comic book characters.

If you have a feeling that a toy is vintage and that you could sell it, try it. The good thing about thrift stores is that they don't charge a lot of money for items. You will stand a better chance of making your money back plus a profit on most of the items you buy and resell. Don't be afraid to take a chance. It might be a better investment than you could have imagined!

Chapter 6- Knowing Whether or Not to Buy

When looking through the endless piles of toys at your local thrift store, you might be confused as to the quality and resale capabilities of the toy. For starters, how do you know if it's simply a thrown out piece of garbage, a knockoff, or a real collector's item? These are tough questions to answer, and it might take you time to figure out exactly what toys you can make some decent money on. In this chapter, I'm going to give you a few tips on what to look for before taking the leap and buying thrift store toys for reselling online.

Quality

As time has progressed, the quality of children's toys has become compromised. Toy companies are more concerned with the volume and their profits. Most toys are now mass produced, taking away from craftsmanship and quality. Take some time to look at the toys that you are considering buying. Are they made from quality materials? Do they seem like they were mass produced? Do they have trademarks or logos on them? By taking a closer look and determining the quality of the item, you stand a better chance at finding a high quality vintage item that can be resold for a good amount of money.

Age

A lot of vintage toys tend to look older. This doesn't mean that they are falling apart. It simply means that they have signs of being loved and used for some time. Along with looking at the quality of the toy's materials, look for signs that the toy has been around for some time. This can be signs such as chipped paint, scratches, or fading. Be careful if the toy is showing signs of damage. The age of the toy can often indicate if it is vintage or not.

Brands

A lot of vintage toys have brands associated with them. Toy brands such as Marx, Playskool, Fisher Price, and other major toy brands have been around for a long time and have a reputation for producing high quality toys. The Marx toys tend to be made of cast iron, making them heavy duty and durable. Playskool and Fisher Price boast a long reputation of making toddler toys that range from blocks to play sets.

Past Popularity

Toys that are based upon movies and cartoons tend to make a comeback if the show was popular during its original time. Take the Teenage Mutant Ninja Turtles for example. They were popular twenty-five years ago and are now coming back, making the original toys popular and collectible.

Look at the Internet

Before going to your thrift store, look on the internet to see what toys are selling well. Try and find those types of toys when shopping. If they are selling well, odds are that you can turn a profit from reselling them yourself. By taking the time to know what sells, you are saving yourself money by not purchasing toys that are not going to give you the maximum profit.

Authenticity

When a toy becomes popular, other companies will try to capitalize on this fact by making similar products. These are not the originals, and they do not hold the same monetary and sentimental value as the original would. By taking a close look at the toy, you will be able to determine whether this toy is one of the originals or one that is made to look like the original so that someone could make some extra money.

Condition of the Toy

The amount of profit that you are able to turn on a toy is highly dependent upon the condition that it is sold in. Since toys often get damaged and altered, make sure that you are taking into account whether or not the clothing and other features of the toy are original. You want to purchase a toy in as close to perfect condition as possible, so major flaws in the toy might be a reason to leave it behind.

When considering your thrift store toy purchase, make sure that you are taking into account the condition and popularity the toys had in the past. The best piece of advice that I can give you is to look closely for markings from the maker of the company that will hint to its originality and value. Also, do your research online before shopping so that you know what will sell and what can be left for someone else to purchase.

Chapter 7- Knowing What to Look for

With so many toys and so many knockoffs out there, it is important to be an informed buyer and seller. Not only will it help you to sell future items, but it will also help your credibility with the online purchasing crowd. The worst thing that you can do is to sell someone a fake when they were expecting the original. Make sure that you are giving the seller what they are expecting and not a toy that closely resembles the original.

Buying thrift store toys is a hit or miss venture. Since you are dealing with items that children have loved and used for who knows how long, you are encountering toys in various conditions. Looking at toys for signs of damage and past repair will be a good way to determine whether or not you can get top dollar for the toy if you were to resell it. If there is too much wrong with the toy, then it might be a good idea to pass it up. People will go for the ones that show the best condition, so if you know that what you're looking at is not in the best shape, then it's likely that you will have trouble selling it.

There is also the possibility of restoring items to their original condition. Depending on the extent of the use and damage of the item, this can either be an inexpensive fix or a costly venture. Remember, you want to make money, not spend it. So, if it looks like a toy is beyond restoration and repair, leave it behind. If the toy is extremely rare, you might still consider purchasing it because collectors will put the time and effort into restoring toys that are rare and worth money. You won't make as much money off the item if you sell it in a less than perfect condition, but it is still possible to make a profit on damaged items.

Another factor that you will want to look for is signs of alterations to the original toy. For example, if you notice that a doll's hair has been cut. The doll will have to be restored in order for it to be in top condition, and replacing a doll's hair can be time consuming and expensive. You know children. They have a sense of creativity that will often be displayed in their toys.

When shopping for vintage toys, the best thing you can do is to be educated on what to look for. This book is just the beginning of the possibilities of what you can find in thrift stores that can be sold for stacks of cash. Another fact about the online world is that it is constantly changing. Some of the toys in this book might be popular now and not be in a year or two. By taking time to research what will sell online will help you to make informed purchases that will benefit your pocket book.

Good luck in your venture into selling thrift store vintage toys online for a profit! I know many people how have succeeded in turning a decent income from this simple task. It only takes a little time to make money! Remember, there are people out there who are looking for the items that sit on your thrift store's shelf. Help you and them by giving them what they are looking for!

Conclusion

Thank you again for downloading this book!

I hope this book was able to help you to identify the toys that you can find and resell online for great profits. Sometimes it is difficult to evaluate whether or not the toy in front of you is vintage and in demand. By knowing what will sell online, you have a good chance at finding toys that will give you stacks of cash.

The next step is to go to your local thrift store and see if you can find any of the toys listed in this book. A stack of cash might be staring back at you from the shelf!

Finally, if you enjoyed this book, then I'd like to ask you for a favor, would you be kind enough to leave a review for this book on Amazon? It'd be greatly appreciated!

TURNING THRIFT STORE ODDITIES AND RARITIES INTO COOL CASH

50 OFF THE WALL ITEMS YOU CAN BUY CHEAP AT THRIFT STORES AND RESELL ON EBAY AND AMAZON FOR HUGE PROFIT

RICK RILEY

Introduction

I want to thank you for downloading the book, Turning Thrift Store Oddities And Rarities Into Cool Cash: 50 Off The Wall Items You Can Buy Cheap At Thrift Stores And Resell On eBay And Amazon For Huge Profit.

This book contains proven steps and strategies on how to take the oddities that you will find in thrift stores and sell them for a profit on Amazon and eBay.

This book is unlike any other book you will find that teaches you how to make money on Amazon and eBay. Most books will tell you about all of the most popular items that you can sell on the sites but that still leaves you with a ton of competition. Other people trying to start their own businesses flipping items they have found at thrift stores.

This book on the other hand is going to teach you how to take those oddities that you will find at thrift stores and flip them for a profit. The items that other flippers would not think of purchasing and reselling, the items that are so often overlooked but sell for a great profit!

This book will help you understand which oddities are going to sell the best and what you need to do to make sure that they reach the right buyers. You will also learn a few selling secrets along the way. I hope you enjoy the book and I hope that it helps you to understand what oddities you will be able to make a profit from.

Thanks again for downloading this book, I hope you enjoy it!

Chapter 1
Strange Finds You Can Profit From

So many people are going to thrift stores and resale shops looking for the best items to sell online. This means that they usually overlook the strange items that you can find and sell for a huge profit. Most of the time people are focused on clothing, antiques and the obvious items that can be found and resold. However, in this chapter you are going to learn about the odd items you can find in thrift stores and sell for a profit.

1. Crazy cat lady figurines. Yes, crazy cat figurines! And no, I am not talking about going out and purchasing 30 tiny cat figurines. There are actually Crazy cat lady action figures that come with several different types of cats. These can be found randomly at thrift stores and they sell very quickly on eBay and Amazon.

2. Miniature log caskets with skeleton. This is a very strange item that people really love to purchase and it is simply a miniature of an old fashioned casket carved out of a piece of wood. Inside the casket you will find a small carved skeleton. Many of these are handmade by random, unknown people and then for whatever reason they end up being donated to thrift stores where they can sell for anywhere from a quarter to fifty cents. Sometimes even less. They can be re-sold very quickly for about $40, depending on the style, with some versions going for even more.

3. Broken vintage and collectible electronics are another odd item that you wouldn't normally think could be re-sold but they are. If you have any type of broken electronics lying around your house that you can no

longer use, just don't have time to fix or don't know how, there is always someone out there looking for these types of items. You can find broken electronics at thrift stores and purchase them for literally pennies and sometimes they will even give these to you. List them and watch them fly off of your virtual shelves.

4. Another highly unusual item that you never would expect to sell are shoes with a sole filled with different random items. They can be filled with glitter, small stones, gems or even tiny doll parts. If you find these at your thrift store make sure to pick them up! I'm seen them sell for up to about $50 a pair. I am not going to claim to know why these items sell but the fact is that they do sell. It may be because they are rare or it could just be that people like the way they look.

5. I honestly cannot explain why this next item would ever sell but it does. Pictures/photos of animals wearing human clothing and taking part in their everyday life. The photos/pictures depict animals doing things such as dogs smoking cigars and playing poker. This is one particular scene often hard to find that will sell very quickly. You don't have to watch specifically for dogs playing poker, it can be cats mowing the lawn or cooking dinner, simply 'pretending' that they are humans.

6. Speaking of pictures and photos, if you come across any spooky, scary paintings in a thrift store, especially if they depict a doll, a child or a clown in a distorted way, they will sell really well. The older and more haunting the painting the higher its value and the more it will sell for. There are a lot of people out there searching for this kind of creepy stuff so while it may be frightening to have to keep it in your home while waiting for it to sell

it's worth it because someone somewhere will pay a lot of money to have it in their collection.

7. Scary masks will also sell very well. They can be Halloween, masquerade or a just an old weird mask of any variety. Just be sure to stay away from cheap masks that you can purchase at your local Walmart, as they are not highly sought after. Instead you want to look for well-made masks. They should look very real and be in good condition. And remember, the creepier that better!

And at the end of day when you are looking for items that you want to sell quickly, you need to look for things that you don't see on a regular basis as well as items that you cannot find at a local store or easily online. And if you ever come across any one of a kind items that means you've really scored! Many times these items will have been hand-made and highly unusual. Those are the items that no one else is going to be able to find!

Chapter 2
Super Strange Items That Bring in Big Money

The following items fall into their own category of "strange". Basically, they are rare items that you really need to keep a watch for while you are in thrift stores. These items tend to be quick sellers on eBay and Amazon as there's always people looking for them. So, although some of them may surprise you they can be a very good investment for your money. And something you can flip and make a profit from.

1. Kool-aid brand sneakers. This is an item that I would never have believed existed if I had not seen it for myself. But just thrift stores sell Adidas and Nike they also sell Kool-aid brand sneakers. Of course, if you are lucky enough to find these shoes you will need to act quickly as they are highly sought after and can be guaranteed to make a profit from.

2. Zombies are all the rage right now and believe it or not, even homemade zombie art can be sold. For example a recent sale was of a lamp that had been turned into zombie art. It had a doll attached to it and it was made to look very scary. This lamp sold for $30! Something like this can be pieced together for around $3 at most thrift stores. Even zombie like cemetery type memorabilia is creepy enough to entice buyers. All things "dead" and eerie will attract the zombie crowd.

3. Furniture made out of animal parts. This is one that may not seem so strange to some but when I say furniture made out of animal parts I mean lamps made

out of deer hooves or chandeliers made out of antlers. There are tons of items like this that you can find on a regular basis if you live in the right area. This is because those who do not live in these areas are willing to pay good money for such items. The same goes for stuffed animals. I don't mean stuffed toys, I am talking about taxidermy items. Like fish that have been mounted, deer heads and any other "stuffed" animals you come across. The only thing you need to check is the size, these can be hard to ship if they are large. You should also check to ensure that the hair is not falling out of the animal, this means it has not been cared for, or preserved properly, and no one is going to want to purchase it.

4. Ventriloquist dummies are something that you should always watch for! These do not have to be strange to sell, in fact if you find these dummies in good condition you will be able to find a buyer for them, but if you find strange looking ones, you will make even more money. As with any item you want to check the condition of the dummies and make sure that they are not falling apart and that they work properly, but ventriloquist dummies are a great find!

5. Junk drawer junk. Watch for items that you would usually find in your junk drawer at home such as old door bells, old remote controllers and such will sell quickly and these items are very easy to ship. Look for small items that people can use on a daily basis, these are guaranteed to sell and you will be able to turn a quick profit.

6. Jewelry is an item that always sells well but you want to again look for items that you cannot find on a regular basis. Items that are unusual as well as rare. These items can be handmade or even wooden pendants from Africa sell very well. Also anything with a gothic theme tends to sell. The creepier and dark the better.

7. African masks are something that you should keep an eye out for. Many people like to hang these on their walls but on occasion they do get donated to thrift stores. When this happens you have a great opportunity to make some quick cash. You may need to clean these up when you buy them and oil the wood, but as long as they are in decent condition you can sell them fairly quickly.

One tip that I want to give you before I finish this chapter is that you need to be very careful when choosing what time you list your items. If for example you are listing at 1 am, your listing is going to be pushed very far down the list by the time anyone wakes up and starts looking for an item. Remember just because you are awake, does not mean that your customers are awake. If you are listing on eBay using the auction style format, always consider what time the auction will be closing as you want to keep as many people actively bidding when it closes.

Chapter 3
All Things Old and Off the Wall Treasures

Of course you can sell many old items for a profit but many people believe that the items you will be looking for are only well known items such as tube radios but that is not true at all. There is a much wider pool of items to buy from when considering selling to the vintage collector.

1. Old photographs always sell well but watch for old photographs that are a bit strange of creepy. Remember there are always those paranormal buffs out there who are looking for items like this. When you look for these photographs make sure that what you are getting is an actual photograph and not a reprint. Of course you can sell reprints, but at $4 each it is going to take a long time for you to make any type of income.

2. Speaking of paranormal buffs if you come across anything that has to do with the world of paranormal while you are out thrift shopping make sure to pick it up. This could be something as simple as an old Ouija board to something as rare as a dybbuk box. Anything will a spiritually dark look to it consider buying. The spookier the better. Many people also list a lot of haunted items but if you want to sell something like that you would have to have some sort of proof, or personal experience with the item being haunted, since there are so many fakes out there and you wouldn't want to mislead someone buying something that's not authentic.

3. Vintage medical instruments are an item that many people will overlook when they are considering which items to list but many of these items will sell very quickly. You need to watch for items that are in good condition as well as in their original box.

4. Clothing is an item that many people do not take the time to even look at when they are in a thrift store, but you should keep your eye out for unusual or rare clothing items. One unusual item that sold on eBay was a loom dress, it actually sold for over $2,000. Keep an eye out for one of a kind items that people have made, these are the items that go for the most money. And when looking at thrift store clothing remember to check

   the pockets! Even the ones inside the coats! You'd be surprised what people leave inside their pockets and forget to check when donating clothes to the thrift store. Many times the thrift store workers are too busy to check each and every pocket and so some tend to get overlooked! And all it takes it one pocket to hold a hidden treasure.

5. Vintage tools with wooden handles are great items to

   sell, but you don't want to list just one item at a time. You will want to keep your eye out for these items when you are shopping and then when you have collected several you can sell them as a lot. Just like the medical tools, there are plenty of people out there who collect these or restore them and are willing to pay a lot of money for such items.

6. Vintage 1980's Hypercolor t-shirts sell for good money on eBay. These are usual multi colored tye dye looking shirts. The special thing about these shirts that make them unique is when the shirt touches heat, it changes colors. These are very popular in the rave culture today. In good condition they usually bring in over $50.

7. Gag gifts are also very popular items and the vintage ones are even more popular. Of course the better the condition of the gag gift, the more money you will get for it. Even simple items such as itching powder and fake poop still bring in money! One item that I find very often is a gag gift called rattlesnake eggs. This item has been around for a long time and I remember playing with it when I was a kid, back then you could get these for about $1 each, today you can sell them online for $20 each and you can sell them all day long!

Keep in mind when you are looking for oddities to sell, you will need to think outside the box. You can actually train your eye to spot these weird kinds of items while you're shopping.

Don't think about what the average person would want because you are not selling items to the average person. It is really good if you can find a niche and work on it for a while before venturing out to other areas. For example gag gifts would be a great place to start or start with paranormal items. Choose a niche that you find interesting and then expand from there.

Chapter 4
Oddities and Wacky Items for Sale

Remember that there is someone out there that will buy anything you list, you just have to make sure they are able to find your listing. I have even seen items such as pine cones sell on eBay. The trick is not to overlook something in the thrift store too quickly. Try to expand your way of thinking and research everything you think is out of the ordinary!

1. Watch for anything with a skull design on it. There are numerous buyers in the rockabilly crowd or retro crowd who love to collect items with this design. This can be a shirt, dress or anything really! There are plenty of people who are looking for these items and you will not be able to keep these items on your virtual shelves.

2. How to books and self-improvement books are also an item that you can sometimes sell very quickly. The ones that sell the best are the older books. The Art of Feminism and books from the 50's is one of the genres people are really looking for. That is not to say you should not keep an eye out for other types like how to draw, paint, etc., as they tend to sell quickly as well. Do some research on what the current pop culture trends are and that can help you zero in on a target market.

Also remember when you're shopping for books, especially old vintage books, to flip through it to see if anyone left anything between its pages. I once found a $100 bill someone had put between the pages of an old Bible! So, you knew know what people tuck away within those covers.

3. JNCO mens vintage 1990's jeans sell great on eBay! These jeans usually have a very wide leg opening at the bottom and a lot of dragon style embroidered artwork on them. They were very popular in the skateboard culture in the 1990's. As a general rule, the larger the size, the more money you can expect to bring in.

4. Vintage McDonalds toys are another item that many people collect. If it came in a Happy Meal at one point in time, then you can bet there is someone out there probably looking for it. You need to make sure that these toys are still wrapped otherwise the chances of selling them are extremely low. I have seen a set of 4 stickers that came in a McDonalds Happy Meal go for $25 just because it was in its original wrapping.

5. Woman's purses are something that can be found in abundance at thrift stores and they are worth taking the time to look at. Purses always sell like crazy online and if you can snag a few good ones here and there you will be able to make a pretty penny off of them. Of course you don't want the average Walmart brand purse, you want something that is rare, old but in great condition or a well-known name. Also, always check inside the purses for items left behind! Just like with old books, people tend to be too busy to check the purses they're giving away to the thrift store and the thrift store workers are sometimes too busy a well to stop and check each and every purse that goes out onto the thrift store floor. And don't forget the zipper compartments! I've found money stashed in the zippered parts of purses before.

6. Keys are something that I find a lot of at thrift stores, but you have to watch for specific keys. You don't want to just purchase a bunch if random keys and expect that

they will sell online. However, if you can find some antique skeleton design keys you will be able to turn a quick profit. Most of the time you will find these and they will look rusted but if you clean them up and treat them with some oil they will look as good as new and will sell fairly quickly.

7.   Military items are also an item that you can sell a ton of and you can sell them very quickly. If you live close to a military base you will be able to find a ton of items at thrift stores there for very cheap. If you can find a uniform with a few patches on it you are going to be able to pull off the patches and sell them alone or you can sell the entire uniform. A lot of time you can find very old uniforms which are very popular, but even if you find something that is not old it is going to sell quickly.

Remember when you are looking for items to sell, the older they are the faster they are going to sell. However that is not to say that newer items will not sell as well. If you come across items that are new, have tags on them or have never been taken out of their boxes, it is worth spending a few dollars on and listing them. If you are able to list an item for about 50 percent or less of what it would cost new, you will be able to sell it.

Chapter 5
Thinking Outside the Collectible Box

I have stated several times in this book that if you want to sell oddities you are going to have to think outside the box and look for items that most sellers would overlook. And one great way to sell several items quickly is to create what's called a "Lot". This is when you sell several items all at once together in one big "group". It is of course best to make sure they all are in the same niche but even if you list a lot of random oddities together in a group chances are someone is going to buy the whole "lot" just so they can get their hands on one specific item within the group.

1. Native American items are also very popular. From peace pipes to moccasins collectors are always looking for these items. You can also watch for dolls that are made to look like Native Americans, paintings, dream catchers and so on. I have always been lucky enough to find several dream catchers when I go out to thrift stores and I have found that even the smallest dream catchers sell very quickly.

2. Always keep your eyes open for the vintage 1980's game called Crossbows and Catapults. This game routinely sells complete for over $150. There were a lot of additional accessories available when the game was popular. Many time you can find the game and also find a lot of the additional accessories included! There are also other vintage games that can bring in high profit.

3. The original NES Nintendo video game system always sells well as you may know. However, be on the lookout for ROB. He was the optional robot that could be purchased with the original system in the 1980's. In complete condition he will typically sell for over $100.

4. Moving on to the subject of glass, there are a few different types of glass items that you should watch for. Cobalt blue glass is very popular right now and if you can find a set of anything made out of this glass you will be able to sell it for a large profit. Hand blown green glass is something that is very rare but you really should watch for. I have found items that I paid $10 for and sold them for over $100 but you need to make sure that the glass is green and not green with another color swirled in or clear with green in it. Pay close attention to the color of the glass. Remember to always check the "new" stock that is coming out from behind the thrift stores closed doors! Keep your eye out for the workers as they bring all the new items from the back of the store. Often times they bring new things out several times a day so it can be worth asking the manager what the best times are to come shopping for the store's "new stock".

5. Fossils are another item that many people overlook and often times these get thrown away when they are given to thrift stores, so you may actually have to ask them to hold on to these items for you. Fossils are worth a lot of money online. The fossil does not have to be something huge, it can be small bird bones fossilized or even a fish. Size does not matter here but the condition of the fossil will. Make sure you know if the fossil is real and what the fossil is of. If you find a replica of a fossil don't worry those sell well also.

6. Anything to do with sports always sells well online but you want to look for items that are rare. Cards that you don't see on a regular basis, magazines about odd sports, even books about sports that are very old and not easy to find can make you a quick profit.

7. Colored vinyl is another thing that I am always looking out for. These records are usually rare and sell for much more than a regular black vinyl record. Even if the colored vinyl is scratched, it can still be purchased and sold for good money as people like to use colored vinyl for different DIY record projects!

8. Postcards and stamps from around the world are another item that you might want to watch out for while you are looking for items to sell. It is wonderful if you can find postcards that have not been written on, but even if they have there are still collectors out there who will want them. We all know that there are people out there who are looking for stamps and the great thing about them is that they are super easy to ship. Just make sure that the stamps have not been used.

9. 80's cartoon lunch boxes can be found at almost any thrift store that you go to and they are very easy to sell online. You can also get quite a bit of money for these if they are in good condition. You have to make sure that you are not paying too much for them. Often times the workers in thrift stores will know what they have when it comes to items like this and will place them under glass instead of out with the other items. Keep your eyes open for lunch boxes that have not been spotted by the workers and get them for as little as possible. Don't forget that when you are purchasing a lot of items it is very easy to talk these workers down on their prices. Don't think that just because an item has a specific price on it that that is what you have to pay for it.

10. Vintage analog synthesizers! As a general rule of thumb, the more knobs the better on the synthesizer. Be careful not to just go out and buy every little Casio keyboard you find. Most often those will not sell very well. If you get lucky enough to come across a Moog or vintage Roland synthesizer in a thrift shop, you can turn a huge profit on it. Always check to see what condition it is in before purchasing.

11. Garbage Pail Kid original stickers from the 1980 are extremely collectible. The better the condition, the more money you can expect to bring in. Some of the cards in the first few series in the mid 1980's bring in big bucks. Many times you can find these in huge amounts jammed in baseball card style boxes.

If you can find an item that is vintage or antique and has at least some beauty to it, then chances are that you can sell it on eBay and Amazon for a profit. Even if the item is not quite beautiful, as long as it has character, you will find someone out there who is looking for that specific item. Never turn an item away just because you wouldn't have it in your own home.

Chapter 6
A Few More Oddities

You may be thinking that it will be difficult for you to find these items at your local thrift stores and although many of them are fairly rare, don't be discouraged! You can find these oddities and other unusual items like them at almost every thrift store that you go to. Chances are that you might have to dig a little to find them because the items may be buried, but trust me they are there to be found! And don't forget when you're shopping to take a quick drive around the back of the thrift store. There you can many times check the trash bins and also ask the thrift store workers if they have any items they'll be throwing away that hasn't make it to the trash yet. Sometimes you just might be surprised what thrift stores throw away and would be willing to give you for free!

1. Salt and Pepper shakers. A lot of people love to collect salt and pepper shakers and although this specific item may not be much of an oddity, you need to keep an eye out for rare, vintage salt and pepper shakers. I recently found one that was a bass jumping out of water, I had never seen a set like this before so I grabbed it for 50 cents, listed it for $20 and sold it within the hour. Salt and pepper shakers like this one that cater to a specific hobby will always sell well. Santa, Easter and other holiday shakers will not because they can be found everywhere.

2. Shadow boxes used to be very popular and many people have started collecting them again. If you can find one that contains little trinkets you will make even more of a profit off of them. I have seen these sell for over $25.

3. Vampires are all the rage right now so if you find anything vampire related you will be sure to make a quick profit. Even something as odd as a doll casket will bring in around $100 so watch for everything vampire!

4. Vintage Christmas items sell great! There is a huge market for vintage Christmas décor. Vintage Christmas ornaments can be bought cheap at thrift stores in the spring and summer and sold for big time money in November!

5. Old empty tobacco tins are an item that seems like it would be garbage but as odd as it may seem, there are those who collect these and are willing to pay a lot of money for these. They do not have to be in the best condition, but of course, like any other item, the better the condition more money you will make off of it. This is a good item for you to collect several of and create a lot to sell.

6. 'Haunted' dolls are really starting to become popular on eBay. The ones that sell are the ones that have the best "creepiest" story attached to it. It isn't so important that the story can be proven but that it's written by a seller who knows how to tell the story well. Now this does not mean you that you should lie and make up stories, but if something you come across has a great history behind it be sure to make it part of the "package" for the buyer!

Chapter 7

A Few More Things to Look Out For

I want to finish up this book by giving you a few more oddities that you can find at thrift stores and sell on Amazon and eBay for a profit. Remember that these are items that most people would not think to sell so chances are you are going to be able to find them in abundance at thrift stores. Most of these are also small so it makes it so much easier to ship than if you were selling fine china or other items that most people try to sell.

1. Chubacabra, mermaids, Bigfoot and all other strange and mythical creatures. You can actually find these items at thrift stores, of course they are going to be some artist's creations but they are great items for you to flip for a profit. Even items such as a cast of a Bigfoot's foot or a mermaid scale will bring in a profit. The reason for this is that people love the strange and unusual and they love to believe that these creatures exist which means that when they have an opportunity to have a piece of these, real or fake, they jump at the chance.

2. Ash trays are something that can always be found at thrift stores but did you know that there are people who are searching for unusual ash trays? You want to be looking for anything that has an unusual theme to it. Also loud designs generally sell great!

3. Canes are another item that a lot of people collect and the stranger the better. So always check the canes and umbrellas out when you are browsing through your favorite thrift store. Once again, try and grab anything

that looks off the wall and unusual. Those designs are what is going to be in demand.

4. Circus items are wonderful items to purchase at thrift stores and you can usually get them at a very low cost and make a huge profit off of them. Anything that has to do with circus freak shows will bring in close to $100 even if it is just a circus flier with the freak show advertised on it. Other circus items that sell very well are old posters and even old ticket stubs. And don't forget to keep your eyes peeled for scary clowns! The creepier looking the better. Those can be especially frightening and you'd be amazed at the large groups of creepy clown collectors there are.

5. The last item that I have for you is any medical book, picture, painting or poster that shows strange abnormalities. For example an old book that shows conjoined twins or one that discusses some of the early and rare medical treatments. Many of these items are extremely sought after because they are so rare and you can bring in a large amount of money with them. Even items that smaller such as a medical illustration from the 16th century can bring in a few hundred dollars!

Those are the oddities that I have for you. Remember that you really can sell anything to anyone. You need to focus on the description of the item, make sure you describe it well and make it sound interesting. Be honest, but remember with many of these historical and off the wall items, 90 percent of the sale is in the description.

Conclusion

Thank you again for downloading this book!

I hope this book was able to help you to discover some oddities that you can look for at thrift stores and sell for a profit on eBay or Amazon.

The next step is to create a list of items that you want to look for on your next trip to the thrift stores and get out there. Find some great oddities to sell on eBay and Amazon. Remember not every oddity is listed in this book so if you find something interesting grab it and take a chance on it!

Finally, if you enjoyed this book, then I'd like to ask you for a favor, would you be kind enough to leave a review for this book on Amazon? It'd be greatly appreciated!

Turning Thrift Store Electronics And Gadgets Into Cash Magic

50 DIFFERENT ELECTRONICS AND GADGETS YOU CAN BUY CHEAP AT THRIFT STORES AND RESELL ON EBAY AND AMAZON FOR HUGE PROFIT

RICK RILEY

Introduction

I want to thank you and congratulate you for downloading the book, *Turning Thrift Store Electronics and Gadgets into Cash Magic: 50 Different Electronics and Gadgets You Can Buy Cheap at Thrift Stores and Resell On eBay And Amazon for Huge Profit.*

This book contains proven steps and strategies on how to turn ordinary electronics and gadgets that you would find at places such as garage sales and thrift stores into profits using eBay and Amazon. Could you use a little extra income, but cannot figure out where to begin? Well, this book is for you!

Electronic treasures are often found at thrift stores and garage sales that people really want to purchase. They will often go to the internet to find such treasures. Why not be the person who could provide their treasure? By knowing how to turn electronics and gadgets into profit, you're not only helping yourself out financially, you are also helping out someone who has been searching for that item. Here's the chance to turn your old electronics and those you find elsewhere into extra cash in your pocket!

Thanks again for downloading this book, I hope you enjoy it!

Chapter 1- Why Should I Use Amazon and eBay?

There are websites out there that offer you the ability to sell your items and make a profit. However, how do you know you're getting the type of service you're looking for? You hear about fraud being committed all the time on websites such as Craigslist, and your first instinct is to take a step back and avoid the internet altogether. However, if used correctly, the internet can be a great resource for buying and selling items. It all depends on where you choose to go.

When I first started selling on the internet, I was leery myself. After all, the horror stories make you want to think twice. However, after doing some research, I have found that using the top websites of Amazon and eBay are quite safe and can help me turn a decent profit.

However, you might have some serious doubts about selling your items online. What if the customer doesn't pay? What happens if you can't sell your item? Well, these websites have you covered on all aspects of the sale. They make sure that you sales are secure and that you get paid what the customer buys it for.

Secure Payment Methods

If you're concerned about disclosing personal information, then you don't have to worry too much because all eBay transactions are handled through PayPal. PayPal is reputable and has been used for years to complete online transactions. So, you have the security of knowing that they will be an efficient method to secure your funds.

Options on How You Want to Sell Your Items

Between the two websites, you can either sell your item outright or put it up in an auction format. This helps you to get the best price for your sale as possible. So, do a little research on your specific item online in order to determine which method would work better for you. You can have accounts on both sites, so don't be afraid to choose one over the other if you think that you can make more with a different sale format.

You also have the opportunity to put your asking price on your item. If the buyer likes how much you're selling it for, then they will buy it. So, when pricing items outright, make sure that you're pricing it fairly and not shorting yourself in the transaction. By looking at similar items, you can get a good idea of how to sell yours.

Less Fraud

Unfortunately, fraud can happen anywhere. However, it seems to happen less on these websites because of the security measures they have set into place. Since they act a middle man for selling goods, you will hardly ever deal with scams from buyers or other sellers concerning your item. This adds a sense of security to the overall experience.

For example, if a buyer wins the auction or buys your item, you don't have to ship it until you're sure you've gotten paid. This takes the risk out of a buyer who simple wants to make your life miserable. Also, both websites offer a great return policy to make sure that a buyer gets what they paid for.

By knowing the benefits of selling on eBay and Amazon, you will feel more confident in posting and selling your items. However, be aware that the websites have to make money, too. So, expect to see fees when selling your items and be prepared to price your items in order to cover the fees that you know will come after the sale!

Once you understand the pros and cons of selling online, you will realize that it is a secure and easy process if you use the right websites. Take some time and evaluate how you would like to sell your items and what type of website will make this possible for you. Remember, you want to make a profit out of your items, so be sure that the method you choose will get you that desired result.

Chapter 2- Best Selling Electronic Items on eBay and Amazon

Now that we have established the benefits to using the websites of Amazon and eBay, we can look at the electronics that will sell on these sites the best. If you're trying to make money selling your electronics, you want to know whether or not they are even worth selling online and whether or not they are in demand by the buying crowd. If your item is in high demand, chances are that you can get a better price for what you're selling. So, without further ado, I'm going to list some of the top selling electronics that top the charts on Amazon and eBay!

Gaming Consoles

Video gaming consoles are always a hot item to resell on the internet. Even if they are older systems, there is still a high demand for them and people who are willing to pay for them. Actually, vintage video gaming systems are collectable and in high demand, whether they are working or not. So, if you come past an old Nintendo in a thrift store, don't be afraid to pick it up and try to resell it. Odds are, you will make a nice profit!

Video Games

Video games for all systems, old or new seem to be a hot item to buy online. However, you need to know a little about the popularity of the game before purchasing it. Some video games just didn't get great ratings, so knowing this will help you to not buy something that won't earn you much of a profit. Games for vintage systems are great sellers as well. Be aware, however, that the games need to by playable and in decent condition in order to get any sort of profit from them online!

Vintage Electronics

If you remember them as a child, chances are that someone is looking for them today. People are constantly looking for electronics that were popular during their childhood. If you come across something like this during your forays in the thrift store, don't be afraid to pick it up if it is selling at a reasonable price. You never know, you might have picked up a treasure and not even know it.

Walkman Cassette Players

Speaking of vintage electronics, name brand Walkmans are in high demand on Amazon and eBay. These can sell for a great profit if they are in great shape and of the right model. If you come across any type of Walkman in a thrift store, pick it up. You might just be finding something that is in high demand that can make you a pretty chunk of change.

Old Telephones

You might laugh, but old corded and cordless telephones are great sellers online. Even though the world has been taken over by cellular phones, people still seek old telephones to add to their homes. With corded phones, the older the phone, the more popular it is. So, if you're looking at an antique rotary phone, it might just be worth it to pick it up and try to sell it!

Lamps and Lighting

Different types of lamps and lighting are nice to sell online. If you're in a thrift store, look for unique and different lighting that might catch a person's eye. People like to have unique elements in their homes, so finding something that suits their style will be a great seller.

Character lighting is another great seller. If you find lamps that feature cartoon or Disney characters, pick them up.

People like to purchase these for children's rooms, and the more unique the piece, the better price you can get for it.

Pinball Machines

Whether it's a table top machine or a full sized pinball machine, these are hot items for people to purchase online. They are also hard to find, so if you have the opportunity to buy one, it will be well worth your time and money to buy it and resell it.

Handheld Video Games

Handheld video games were a huge item for children in the 1990s. Today, they are collector's items and they sell very well on the internet. Take some time and look out for some of these old games and pick them up when you have the chance. They could be little gold mines waiting to happen.

On the other hand, handheld gaming consoles, such as the Nintendo Gameboy Classic, is also a top seller online. These are also difficult to come by, so finding one in any condition is a treasure.

IPod

IPods of all generations can make a nice chunk of change on eBay and Amazon. Even if the unit isn't functional, people will buy these for their parts. The classic IPods tend to get the most money because they carry a higher capacity for storing music. However, the IPod touch is up and coming. So, no matter how old the IPod, it is a good investment to purchase it. If the model is no longer made, it might be in higher demand than the ones that are still readily available in stores.

Used Cell Phones

Used cell phones, especially smartphones, are a great item to resell online. As the technology advances, people will go for the new and get rid of the old. However, these old phones are still quite usable and still have a lot of life left in them. People will go to the internet to find deals on cell phones, so take advantage of this crowd and snatch up functional used cell phones when you see them!

Cameras

Different types of cameras can be worth a ton of money. If you're not knowledgeable with cameras, you might be passing by a great deal on a professional quality camera that has lenses that might sell for a lot of money. Film cameras are now becoming an item of the past and people seek them wherever they can find them. Think about it. If you go to the store to purchase a camera, you will very rarely find film cameras on store shelves. Use this to your advantage and when you find one, pick it up and sell it online!

Computers

Refurbished computers are a hot item online. Buying a new computer is costly, so people will often seek out computers that have been previously used and restored. If you have experience with computers, you might even be able to tweak a computer with desired elements that someone would be willing to pay money for. When you come past a computer in a thrift store, take into account its age and its capability to be resold. Even vintage computers can be resold for profit, so don't discount a computer simply because it's outdated.

Televisions

If you come across old tube televisions, these are in high demand amongst collectors. Since they are no longer made, people have started to collect them and the prices for an old tube television have risen drastically. On the same score, new televisions that are way underpriced at a thrift store can also bring a good price when resold online. So, just because you encounter a television at thrift store, don't think that it is total trash. People do donate items that they simply have no use for.

Portable Audio

Just like Walkmans are selling for high prices online, other forms of portable audio will also get a good price. For example, old portable cd players are in high demand among collectors. You have to be careful with these though because many of them that are donated are no longer operational. You might still be able to sell it for parts, but for the most part, a dead portable cd player is virtually worthless.

Other portable audio that can be sold online for great prices include any type of MP3 player. Having the capability to take music and media on the go is huge among the general public. So, take some time and look through the smaller items in this section. You never know what you might find.

Tablets

Within the last couple of years, tablets have taken over the electronics world. People like these because they function as a miniature computer without the hassle of carrying around a laptop. The fact that they are extremely portable is their best selling point. There are many different brands of tablets that are being sold, so make sure that you know which brands are good and which ones have lower ratings. You might waste your money if you buy a tablet that nobody wants because of bad ratings.

Vintage Calculators

In the world of collectors, old calculators have great value. Many of these are the older model graphing calculators. Certain models will sell of more on the market than others, so if you're looking to buy a used graphing calculator, check out which models are in highest demand.

Electronics make peoples' lives easier. So, when they are good or if they have collectible value, they can often get a great price when resold. Remember, not every person is able to find what they are looking for electronics-wise, so you might just be offering them something that they have been desperately searching for! Just because it has no value to you doesn't mean that it doesn't have value to someone else.

Chapter 3- How to Find These Items Wherever You Are

Before I go to the thrift stores, I check out the top selling items on the websites that I hope to sell on. Most of the top websites, including Amazon and eBay have lists of items that have been selling more than others within a certain time period. Take note of the types of items that seem to be selling and keep an eye out for them when you are making your rounds to thrift stores.

Depending on the area you live in, you have different chances of finding some items than others. For example, you might find newer electronic items in areas where the population has a higher income. They have the money to be able to update their electronics more frequently than those who don't have a higher income. So, if you're looking for these types of electronics, go to thrift stores in the areas that cater to the higher income population.

You might give other thrift stores a chance and see what you can find. People donate items that you might not expect them to donate. Don't discount a thrift store based upon the surrounding demographics. Give even the most remote thrift stores a chance.

Tips for Finding Good Electronics in Thrift Stores

If you're leery of finding decent electronics in a thrift store, you're not alone. Many electronic items that are donated are often broken or unusable. This makes it difficult to resell them. How do you make sure that you're getting an item that can be resold for a decent price? Well, let's take a look at some ways that you can know if you're getting ripped off or getting a deal.

Testing Stations

In the past few years, I have noticed that a lot of the thrift stores have an area where you can test the electronic equipment so you know what you're buying before you actually purchase it. This can really work to your benefit because you can get idea if there are some small flaws with the equipment that can be looked past or if there is something that cannot be fixed whatsoever and you would be better leaving it behind. So, take advantage of the electronics testing stations in the thrift stores if they are offered.

Look at the Physical Condition

Sometimes the outward physical appearance of the electronic item can give you an idea of if there is something wrong with it working. If it's a highly sellable item, test it if possible. Often if the item has major external damage, it is damaged within. However, it can still have internal faults and still look okay on the outside. Use your judgement if you have doubts about the item.

If the Price is Right, Buy it

Even if the item appears to be damaged, if it is being sold for a relatively inexpensive amount, don't hesitate to purchase it.

The worst that can happen is that you cannot resell it. If it's a big item, make sure you do your inspection thoroughly before buying it. The item might seem overpriced, so wait it out if you feel that it would resell for a higher price. Thrift stores always have sales!

By knowing what you're buying and its condition, you stand a better chance at getting the most money out of it when it's resold. Finding the items can be the most difficult of the operation, so once you get past that, you are ready to go online and sell. Happy shopping!

Chapter 4- Gadgets that Sell Well on eBay and Amazon

High end electronics are not the only items that can sell on eBay and Amazon. Smaller electronics and gadgets can also resell for some good profits. These items are often easier to find in thrift stores and won't cost as much as the higher end electronics. However, just like the other electronic items, you must be careful about their condition and pricing. Here are some of the small electronics and gadgets that can be sold for good profits on the internet.

Wireless Routers

Any type of wireless router can be resold for a profit. Since buying a router new is expensive, people often turn to eBay and Amazon for better prices. Knowing this, when you find an operational router at a thrift store, know that someone out there is looking for a deal on one and might not think to go thrift shopping themselves.

GPS Systems

GPS systems are becoming increasingly popular since people tend to go more places and need directions. Finding a good GPS can be hard, but if you find one in a thrift store, you can easily resell it at a bargain to someone looking for that device!

Go Pros

Fitness is taking on new levels with the new devices out there to record and monitor your activity levels. Go Pros have become very popular because they are hands free and can take amazing video while the person is performing the task. Since these devices are rather pricey, if someone can find a deal on them online, they will buy them.

DVD and Blue Ray Players

Used DVD and Blue Ray players are a hot item if they are of a good brand and in good condition. Anyone can go and buy a new DVD player for cheap, but a good name brand player in good condition is more than likely going to sell better when resold online.

Adapters for Apple Products

Since most Apple devices only come with the cord that hooks into your computer, wall chargers and car chargers for Apple devices are great items to resell online. Since Apple is such an exclusive brand, their adapters and chargers tend to be expensive when bought brand new.

Record Players

Records are popular among collectors, so it stands to reason that old record players would be popular as well. However, you need to make sure that they are in good operational order. If you do try and resell one with defects, make it known in the listing. Most people don't want to buy broken devices.

Digital Recorders

Digital recorders can be bought for a low price and resold for a higher price online. Students and others like to have these devices for recording lectures and not having to take massive amounts of notes.

MP3 Players

As mentioned before, IPods and other MP3 players are popular for reselling online, despite their condition. People will often buy broken MP3 players for the parts to fix another player. Depending on the brand and the storage capacity, these can be resold for a nice profit.

Car Electronics

Car speakers and radios sell well online if they are of a quality brand. You need to know which car electronics brands are top notch in order to make a good investment when you see them sold at thrift stores.

Accessories for Popular Electronics

Accessories for cell phones and other electronics sell very well online. The better the condition and the brand name, the better the price you can resell it for. This can include headphones and microphones as well as webcams and other accessories for computers.

Surveillance Equipment

With safety being a concern for many families, surveillance equipment has become a hot item to be bought online. From cameras to keypads to set alarms in homes, people want to feel safe and are looking for the equipment to do so.

Cable Alternative Devices

In the past year or so, Amazon and other online companies have come up with ways to get premium programming without going through a cable company. A lot of these are in the form of a stick that will plug into your television and work with your internet connection.

Headphones

High end headphones will sell well online because it is less expensive to purchase them online rather than buying them new. Make yourself familiar with the top brands and look for them when shopping.

DVDs and Blue Ray Discs

With the prices of new discs rising in stores, people will seek out their movies on used discs. Depending upon the movie, its rarity and popularity, you can actually make a good profit by reselling these online. Thrift stores price them all the same, so they really don't take into account the titles or the condition of the discs.

Power Tools

Name brand power tools can be easily bought and resold if in good condition. Know what the top selling brands are and what models sell the best. When people buy used power tools, they look for the newer models, so if it looks older, it's probably not going to sell well.

Printers

Top brand printers and printer accessories are good to resell online. However, you must make sure that they are in good working order. People tend to look for top selling brands, so be aware of this when looking at these. The lower level brands can be bought new at cheap prices, so many people will buy them new. Don't waste your money on a cheap printer that you won't be able to resell.

Photo Printers

People like to print their own photos from the comfort of their home, so photo printers have become increasingly popular. These too can be pricey if purchased new, so people look for good quality used ones online.

Computer Software

Used and new computer software can be sold online as long as they are not outdated and the discs are in good condition. You also want to be aware that you're looking for the more popular software and not the stuff that no one has heard of before.

Vacuum Cleaners

Top name vacuum cleaners are also a great seller online as they are very expensive if bought at a retailer. Look for the top brands and make sure that they operate well before reselling them.

Kitchen Appliances

Small kitchen appliances such as blenders, microwaves, toaster ovens, and food processors are in high demand and people will search for and buy them online.

Small gadgets and electronics can be great sellers if they are priced right for the buyer and are in decent condition. People often turn to eBay and Amazon because they can find what they are looking for at a reduced price. Even if the item is used, they are still getting a bargain and are happy not to have to pay full price for the item. Keep this in mind while shopping for items to resell online. Think like a buyer would and you will find that you're buying items that can easily be resold.

Chapter 5- Knowing How to Price Your Items

Once you have your items, you might wonder how you can price them so that you are making money and the buyer is going to purchase it. This takes a little research and knowledge on your part. Not every item is going to sell for the same price. Since you are buying these items at a thrift store, they are more than likely going to be used and have a various array of defects. You have to take this into account when you price your item online or start the bidding for the item on eBay.

Look at Similar Items

Go onto the internet and look at what your item is selling for on eBay and Amazon. Both of these websites list the popular items and how much they sold for within the last day or so. You want to keep your pricing within the same range as similar items. If it is overpriced, you stand the chance of not being able to sell it and if you price it to cheap, you won't make much, if any, profit off of it.

Evaluate the Condition of Your Item

Since you are reselling a used item, you must take into account the damage and flaws that the item might have. These can range from scratches to small operating malfunctions. Depending on how good of shape the item is in, you can price it accordingly. People aren't going to buy something knowing that it has damages if they can get the same thing without the damage.

What did You Pay for it?

Keep in mind how much you paid for the item. You are trying to make a profit, so you don't want to lose money in the resale process. Price your items and start the auctions off to ensure that you are making money from your resale and not losing money or wasting time because you broke even. This might happen a few times, but being aware of the items original sale price will make it easier for you to price it to make a profit.

Allow for Shipping Costs

When you price your item, you have to take into account the shipping costs. More than likely, the buyer will pay this, but you must set the rate that they will pay for it to be shipped.

Make sure that you're allowing for a shipping cost for foreign sales because you can end up losing money if a foreign buyer purchases your item and you quote them the domestic shipping price.

At first, pricing used items can seem a little overwhelming, but knowing the condition of the item and how much similar items have sold for recently will help you to make a reasonable price for your item. By taking time to do a little research on the specific item and knowing what a fair price is for it, you will be better prepared to price it so that you make a profit and that it will sell quickly.

Chapter 6- How to Buy These Items in Thrift Stores

Thrift store shopping can be sensory overload for those who haven't done much of it in the past. However, when you get the hang of the shopping, you can easily find items to resell without feeling overwhelmed. Taking a structured approach to your shopping will make it much easier for you to get in and out and find what you're looking for. In this chapter, I'm going to give you a few hints on how to shop in thrift stores and get them at a bargain so that you can make a larger profit when reselling them.

Seek Items with Sale Stickers

Most thrift stores will price their items using different colored stickers. On certain days of the week, these stickers are half off, making the item an even better deal. Know which color is on sale that day when you're in the store and try and find items with these tags if at all possible.

Use Coupons

Some thrift stores will issue percent off coupons when you make a donation to the charity that they support. By combining these coupons with the low prices that the store offers, you can save even more money on the items that you're looking at.

Know What You're Looking for

One way to keep yourself from being overwhelmed is to know what you're going to look for even before you enter the store. If it's going to be video games, then focus on finding video games to resell. Don't let the store distract you. If you see other electronics that would be good for resale, don't be afraid to look at them as well. By being able to go straight for the area that you're planning on looking in, you will save yourself time and stress. Also, by knowing the specific type of item you want to focus on will help you to narrow down your search even more.

However, if the store you're in doesn't have the type of item you're looking for, it doesn't hurt to browse the section and see if there are any other items that would be useful for resale. You don't have to have a wasted trip even though you didn't find exactly what you were looking for.

Shop during Sale Days

If you want to make a larger profit, then going to a thrift store during a large sale day is another option. You will be dealing with more people, but if you know what you're looking for, you won't feel stressed out by the extra bodies in the store. Thrift stores tend to put their entire inventory on sale at least once a month. By knowing when these sales are, you stand a good chance at getting your item at a great price.

Know Your Thrift Store

At first, you're not going to know the layout and the policies of the thrift stores that you're shopping in. After a while, you will be able to go straight to the area that sells what you're looking for and be able to look through the inventory quickly and efficiently. Since thrift stores stock what is donated, their inventory constantly changes, so frequent visits are to your benefit.

Knowing your thrift stores and how to shop them during sales is going to be a great way to maximize your profit-making potential. Many people don't know how to shop during sales and end up spending more than they would if they were focused on the tags and dates. If you shop more than one store, keep a calendar of the sale dates so that you make sure you hit them for an opportunity to make the best profit when you resell your items.

Chapter 7- The Secrets to Turning Your Finds into Profits

Even though it takes some time and effort to get your business started selling electronics on eBay and Amazon, it will be worth it once you get the hang of it and know what to expect. From actually buying the item to selling and shipping it can seem like a long and drawn out process, but once you have a routine, it will seem easy and efficient.

At first, you're not going to know what you're looking for and what to look for. It takes time and research in order to find items that you can make into profits. Another factor that might inhibit you from making the most out of your reselling is that you don't know how to sell them. Selling on the internet is based on description and pictures. You must have both of these in order to make your item stand out.

Once you get good at pricing and finding items to sell, you will be well on your way to making great profits online. Since pricing can be tricky, learning how to price your items so that you make the most money and are attracting customers can have a find balance. This will take time and skill to perfect. Sometimes you're going to take a loss, but the ultimate goal is to make more money than what you spent on the item.

The great thing about reselling thrift store items is that you don't invest large amounts of money to buy your merchandise. If it doesn't sell or it turns out to not be worth what you thought, you're not taking a huge financial loss. After some time, you will become an expert at finding resale items that will earn you the maximum profits. Don't be disappointed if you don't see the profits come in right away.

Last of all, know what your customer is looking for. By catering to the people, you will be successful when reselling your items. You can find out what is popular by looking at eBay and Amazon and knowing what people are buying. Take some time to know what to look for and what people ultimately will pay for.

Good luck and happy selling!

Conclusion

Thank you again for downloading this book!

I hope this book was able to help you to know what to look for when buying thrift store electronics to resell on eBay and Amazon. Electronics can be a tricky area to find decent and profitable items for resale, so knowing what to look for will be a great advantage to making maximum profits.

The next step is to take the steps in this book and go into a thrift store and find electronics you can sell for a profit. Knowing what to look for and what a fair price is are the first steps in making a nice profit.

Finally, if you enjoyed this book, then I'd like to ask you for a favor, would you be kind enough to leave a review for this book on Amazon? It'd be greatly appreciated!

Thrifting
and
Winning

50 WAYS TO MAKE MONEY BUYING ITEMS AT THRIFT STORES AND SELLING THEM FOR HUGE PROFITS

RICK RILEY

Introduction

I want to thank you for downloading the book, *Thrifting and Winning: 50 Ways to Make Money Buying Items at Thrift Stores and Selling Them for Huge Profits.*

This book contains proven steps and strategies on how to find items in your local thrift store and resell them for maximum profits. Thrift stores are a treasure chest of items that are just waiting to be found. For some, it's only junk, but for others, it can be a gold mine.

When looking at a thrift store, don't look at it as someone else's used junk, but look at it as a way to find treasures to make you extra money. People will donate items that are worth tons of money on a daily basis. Why not capitalize on these treasures? This book will help you to find these items and sell them in such a way that you can make tons of cash from your local thrift store. Let's make some money!

Thanks again for downloading this book, I hope you enjoy it!

Chapter 1- Thrift Stores: A World of Possibility

If you're like a lot of people, you might view thrift stores as a place where people recycle their used junk. Much of these items are old and damaged, but someone will be able to use them, right? You may not realize that you can actually find some wonderful treasures in the aisles of these stores. People give away items that they may not know are valuable on a daily basis. If they are uninformed about what they hold in their hands, it's their loss and your gain.

Being able to find items in the thrift store that are worth money will take some time and research. Since not many people take the time to know what they have within their possession you can definitely use your knowledge to benefit you financially. Just think of what you can find within the walls of your local thrift store if you would have the time and the knowledge to find out!

Now that you know that your local thrift store is a great place to make some money, it's time to figure out what you can find there that will earn you that extra cash. Learning what people are looking for and would spend money on will help you get the edge on finding the items and making top dollar on them.

If you're still uncertain as to what this would look like, don't worry. We will take a look at the top items for you to look for as well as methods to ensure that you are getting the most money from them.

Millions of items go through thrift stores on a daily basis that the people buying and donating them don't have any clue as to what their true worth is. With an opportunity like this, why not take advantage of the lack of knowledge in this area? By educating yourself and knowing what you as an individual can look for when thrift store shopping, you can potentially earn major cash by finding the right items in your local thrift store!

Looking at your thrift store in a different light will give you some inspiration and excitement to get started on this venture. You may have some difficulties to begin with, but once you get started, you will find that you will develop a method for finding what you can make the most money on and finding the best way to earn this money.

Let's get started on tips for finding thrift store items to resell for big money! This might be the way you can make extra income that you have been searching for!

Chapter 2- What to Look for in Thrift Stores that is Worth Money

If you have not had many experiences with thrift stores, the thought of suddenly going into them and trying to find something of worth can be like trying to search for a needle in a haystack. The size of most thrift stores can make it an all-day venture if you don't know what you're looking for and how you can cut corners to find it. Taking the time to know what you can find in your thrift store will ultimately save you time when you walk through the doors and see just how much stuff is on the shelves.

What can you find in a thrift store to make you some extra money? That is probably the burning question in your mind right now. Getting started might take a little time, but once you have learned the methods for finding what you can use, you will begin to find a system that will work well for you.

Look for Top Brands

Every genre of items has a popular brand name label. From clothing to electronics, there will be brands that will stand out from the rest of the pack. Knowing which brands are the top brands and how much they are really worth can help you to search through the shelves and racks with a more scrutinizing eye. You are not looking for aesthetically pleasing items as much as you are looking for who made them. Top brands will often sell for more money than their less popular counterparts, so keep that in mind as you do your searching and research.

Look at the Age of the Item

Older looking items can be either well used or antiques. Knowing when you find an antique can help you to find items that will be collectable amongst a certain crowd. Since many older items are no longer made, when people come across them, they will want to purchase them for their collections. If you are going in search of antique or collectable items, know what you're looking for and know that antiques can look older in respect to other items that you might encounter.

Look at the Material the Item is Made From

The materials that items are made of can help to determine their value. Higher quality and rarer materials are worth more than cheaper made materials. For example, if you're looking at figurines, the ones that are made with porcelain will be worth more than the ones that are made of simple clay. By knowing the difference in these materials, you can pick out what you would believe to be higher valued items from those that are not worth much at all.

Know What is Popular

Even if the item may seem silly and not worth the time to look at, it may be incredibly popular amongst a group of collectors. Kids will have fads that you think are ridiculous, but those who are a part of the fad will pay top dollar to get whatever the fad requires. Take a look at current trends and try to find items that will fit into the popular trends. They can make you much more money than not knowing what people out there are looking for.

Search Online Websites to See What is in Demand

Along with knowing what is popular, you can use your resources to find what people are looking for. The internet is a wonderful resource. You can look on the popular auction and sales websites to see what people are actually buying. This can help guide you when you go into a thrift store and have no idea where you would like to begin.

Learn to Look After the New Merchandise is Put Out

Thrift stores will have certain times when they will move their new inventory out to the sales floor. This is a prime time to look at what they have to offer because not too many people have had the chance to look through it before you get there. This will help you to have a better chance at finding the best items you can sell without having to do a lot of digging.

Visit Multiple Stores

Different areas and neighborhoods will have different types of items donated to their thrift stores. By looking in multiple thrift stores in different areas, you will get to see a better array of what the thrift store world can offer you. If you have extra time, try going to the different areas within your city or another nearby city and see what you can find!

Look Behind the Items in Front

With so many donations being dropped off, some of the items will get pushed back on the shelves to make room for the new items. By taking the time to look at the items that have been pushed to the back, you can find some treasures that people will pass by because they will just look at the items in front.

Scrutinize Grab Bags Carefully

When there are a lot of items that serve a similar purpose, such as office supplies, thrift stores will often combine these into bags and sell the entire bag at a certain price. Valuable items can be tucked in these grab bags because the employees who put them together may not know what they have in their hands is really valuable. It might take a little extra time, but finding the treasure in a grab bag can be totally worth it.

By knowing where to get started and what to look for in a thrift store, you will be better prepared to go in and find the items that can be useful to you. Before going into the store, try looking around and finding out what items are valuable and what brands are in demand. You can save yourself a lot of time and frustration by doing just a little research before going in!

Chapter 3- Finding Websites and Other Venues to Sell Your Goods on

Once you have found the items in the thrift stores, it's time to make the next move and sell your finds to the people who will want them. However, there are different ways in which you can sell these items. Some ways will earn you more money than others, so knowing which ways to sell certain items will help you to get the most out of the items that you have found.

Where can you sell used items? How can you find the customers who will pay top dollar for what you have? These are the questions that you might be asking yourself at this very moment. Don't worry, you're not the only one! Let's take a look at the different ways you can sell your thrift store finds for the most money.

eBay

eBay is the top auction website on the internet. Anyone can buy or sell on this site, and many people will turn to this site first when looking for items that they are seeking. However, some items will sell better in this setting than others. Collectibles and popular items are huge sellers on this website. Think about selling items such as toys, trading cards, and unique figurines when selling on eBay. The bidding will work the price up and you may be surprised with how much your item will sell for in the end.

Amazon

Amazon is another popular site where sellers can offer their wares. This site is set up with you choosing how much you would like the buyer to purchase your item for. In order to do that, you will need to know what your item is worth and not overpricing it. Also, you will want to ensure that you are pricing it with its condition in mind. Many people will turn to Amazon to look for used books and music. You may find that other items that you have found will sell well in this setting too.

Antique Stores

If you're dealing with items that are older and may be out of production, an antique store may be the place to sell your finds in. Large antique shops operate by renting out areas where people can set up their own shops. In order for this to be a possibility, you will want to have a wide array of items that would be considered antique. If you don't then you may want to consider partnering with another seller and renting a booth together.

Craft Fairs

If you are dealing with items that can be considered crafty, such as wall art or quilts, then a craft fair could be a great way to get top dollar for your items. Again, like an antique store, craft fairs are operated in booths, so you will want to make sure that you have more than a few items to sell in order to make this worth your while.

Craigslist

Even though many people are afraid of buying and selling on Craigslist, you can actually make a decent amount of money on this site if you're careful and know how to avoid fraud and dangerous situations. This is a good site to sell the larger items on, so think about using it if you find high quality furniture that you know that someone will be looking for.

Etsy

If you don't have enough merchandise to sell at a craft fair, Etsy is the craft fair's online counterpart. You can individually list your items on this website and sell as few or as many items as you wish. This site operates much like Amazon, except it deals with handmade goods. So, if you have a few crafty items you wish to sell and don't want to go through the hassle of a craft fair, consider opening an using an Etsy account to sell them!

Social Media

Many social media sites have groups that have come together to buy and sell in certain areas and certain types of items. You can easily search these groups and find one that your items would fit into and ask to join the group. After admitted, you can post your items and sell it to the people within the group.

Knowing where you can sell your items and which ways to sell your items will ensure that you get the best price for what you sell. Before posting or setting out your items, take a look at what the store or the site has to offer. If you see that similar items sell well in one area and not in another, go with the best way to sell what you have. You can also use several of the methods to sell different types of items. The more you understand about where to sell, the better chance you have of making a better profit.

Chapter 4- Learning to Ask the Appropriate Price

One of the biggest mistakes that new sellers make is not pricing their goods appropriately. Some will severely overprice their items and no one will purchase them, or the seller will underprice the item and take a small profit or a loss from what they sell. Knowing how to find the best price for your items will take some research, but knowing what you can get for what you have will benefit you in the long run.

How do you price used items? You might feel awkward pricing something that you just purchased used. Why would anyone buy something used from you? You would be surprised at how well used items really do sell. In this chapter, I'm going to give you some tips on how to price your items just right to make sure you get the best profits from your items.

Search the Web for Similar Items

Since the internet is a great way to find out information, use it to your benefit. When going onto the internet to research which method would be best for selling your item, look at the asking prices of other sellers. This can give you a general idea of how much the item can sell for. Also, you can look and see what similar items have already sold for on some of the sales websites. Gather this information and use it when pricing your own item. You want to ask a fair price without asking too much or too little.

Use Antique Pricing Catalogs

If you're dealing with antiques, pricing guides can be a wonderful resource for you when pricing what you wish to sell. These guides will tell you how much the item will sell for by year and condition. The prices given are the average price that you can buy them for, so if you price what you're selling within those limits, you should be able to get a good price for what you're selling.

Find a Good Pricing Guide

Pricing guides are out there for almost anything that you wish to buy or sell. Find the appropriate and most up to date guides and use them as a reference when selling your items. These guides are written by the experts, so you know that the advice is reliable and that you won't get taken advantage of.

Look for Trends in Pricing

As time goes on, some items will change in popularity and demand, therefore changing how much you can sell it for. If the price of what you're selling takes a dive, you don't want to keep asking that high of a price for it. Lower or raise your price according to what the current pricing trends are.

Note the Item's Condition When Pricing

When dealing with used merchandise, there is always the question of the item's physical condition. Your buyers will want to know what that condition is when you sell it. If it's not in factory packaging, you need to give as much detail about the item as you can, and you need to let the price that you're asking for the item reflect that item's condition.

Price Competitively

In order to actually sell your item, you don't want to ask top dollar for it. You want to entice the buyers to purchase what you're selling. So, price your item like the other ones of the same condition, but make buyers come to yours because you can give them the best price. This is a good idea, especially if you're dealing with an auction website or another website that expects you to sell your item in a certain time frame.

If Auctioning, Start Low

When using sites such as eBay, start your initial bid low and let the buyers work it up for you. If you start with a minimum bid that is too high, then people will find similar items to bid on instead. People will want to get the cheapest price for what you have to sell, and if they feel if they can get that elsewhere, your item may not sell at all.

Pricing your items is an incredibly important element of getting the most out of your thrift store finds. Finding a good price and having people think that it is reasonable are the best ways to ensure that you sell what you want for what it is really worth. Don't allow the buyers to dictate the price if you know that it is worth more than they are willing to pay. It might just mean that you have to find a different way to sell it.

Chapter 5- Know When You're Being Taken Advantage of

As I have mentioned before, you want to sell your item for top dollar, and your buyer wants to purchase it for as little as possible. When these factors come into play, you can easily fall into the buyer's hand. However, you can counteract the problem by knowing what the true value of your item is, and you can know what you can reasonably sell it for. There will be people out there who will try to get you to sell it to them for less. Some of them can be very convincing. You can combat these types of people by knowing how to stand up for yourself in the selling world.

How confident are you that you won't let people take advantage of you? If you feel like people do that in your life, it's time to look at ways that you can avoid being made a fool of and losing money instead of taking away a profit.

Know What Your Item is Truly Worth

By doing your research and knowing how to price your items fairly, you shouldn't have to haggle the price with a potential buyer. The price should sell it for what you want to sell it for. People will constantly try to get more for less, so stand up for yourself and don't let them get away with getting what you have to sell for less than you know you can sell it for.

Be Polite When Discussing Prices

You will get people who will want to discuss buying your item, but they will want to buy it for what they want to buy it for. If you know that what they are willing to give you is much less than what you know you can get for it, be polite and let them know that they can either purchase it for the asking price or not purchase it at all.

Be Aware of Private Messages on Sales Websites Concerning Pricing

If using an auction website, you might get private messages from bidders asking you to sell it to them for a certain price. While other bidders are honestly bidding on your item, someone is trying to get in and get it without having to deal with the competitive aspect of the site. More than likely, your auction price will get you more than this secret buyer is willing to pay. So, just be polite and let this buyer know that the item can be purchased by the highest bidder.

Stick to Your Price

If you know that the price that you have given your item is fair, then don't let anyone try to haggle it down. The item will sell for what you want it to if it is in demand and you have set a fair price on it. Remember, people are trying to get more for less, so don't fall victim to their whims. Stick to your price and don't let them tell you what you should sell it for. You have done your research and you're sticking to it!

Know When You Should Give in

Sometimes, no matter how well you price your item, it will not sell for what you wish it to sell for. This can be due to a number of reasons, but it is better to get something from your merchandise than not to be able to sell it at all. If you have a buyer who is interested and can give you what you at least paid for it, then give in and let that item go. It might just be that your item wasn't what you thought it was and you shouldn't waste any more time on it.

Don't Take Payments Outside of Cash or PayPal

There are a lot of scams out there. Sadly enough, people will use alternative methods of payment that are often fraudulent when purchasing items. Don't allow that to happen to you. When selling your items in person, accept only cash. You can verify if the cash is real by looking at its security features. If selling online, use a reliable third party, such as PayPal. They will protect you from cyber fraud.

Knowing a Scammer When You See One

Scammers can be smooth characters. They might seem like the nicest and most honest people, but that is a ploy to get what they want. Look for things that just don't fit when you're dealing with a potential buyer. Often times, your gut feeling can lead you to make the right decision regarding your sale. Listen to your gut and don't sell it if the buyer seems off in any way. There will be other people out there who will buy what you have to sell.

Be Aware When Someone Offers You More Than You Know the Item is Worth

Sometimes, a scammer will try to give you more for what you're selling than what it is really worth. This is a way for them to get what you have to sell and also take advantage of you. When you try to tell them that they are offering too much, they will ask for you to send the extra money back. In reality, that money was bogus to start with.

Being taken advantage is not fun. When you're trying to be honest and make an honest income, getting scammed can really hurt. People will take advantage of you if given the chance. Even if you like to think the best of people, be careful. They might just be putting on an act to get what they want for what they want it for, and you will take the loss in the end.

Chapter 6- Learning to Find Opportunities in Your Community

Every community has different events and opportunities to buy and sell. While one community can be on the internet, another one can be your local church or charity group. Finding opportunities in your community to buy and sell will help you to make even more money. Even if you stick to thrift stores, you can find areas in your community that you can sell your finds in.

If you're looking for other opportunities to purchase items to sell for a profit, community events can also be a helpful place to start. Knowing your community and its offerings well can help you get an edge on making the most money from your finds! Don't limit yourself to just thrift stores. You can use other resources to find items that will earn you major cash right in your community. Your community can also help you with selling the items.

Church Garage Sales

Church garage sales are a prime place to find items of worth. You can navigate these much the same way as you would navigate a thrift store, and you can often get the price lower than what they want for it. Also, you are supporting the community by buying from an organization within the community. Garage sales also tend to ask lower prices of items than you would pay for them in a thrift store. If you can get it at a garage sale, you might get a better bargain and a better profit from your purchase in the end.

Community Garage Sales

A lot of housing developments and smaller towns often have one huge garage sale in which multiple people participate. This can give you the opportunity to walk around and find things that may not end up in the thrift stores. Just like a church garage sale, the owners might let you haggle them down on the price just to get rid of the items. Take advantage of this when going to the garage sales. You can use the same knowledge that you used for the thrift stores when wandering someone's garage sale.

Another great thing about garage sales is that people are bound and determined to get rid of their junk. They might take any price for it rather than having to load it and take it to the thrift store. Knowing the characteristics of garage sales can work to your advantage, especially if you know that the item that you are purchasing can earn you some major cash!

Local Antique Shops

Local antique shops could be a great way for you to sell your antiques that you purchased at the thrift store. They are looking for inventory too, and they wish to bring in customers. See if they are willing to give you a good price for the items that you are selling and allow them to deal with the retail end of the bargain.

Also, if you can build a relationship with a local antique shop owner, they might allow you to sell your items in their store for a small fee. When looking into this, you can make more money because you are not having to deal with people haggling you and you don't have to worry about paying shipping and handling fees for your items!

Message Boards

There might be areas in your downtown area where people can post their flyers and ads. Try using this method and post your item to sell it. This works out well in college areas because students like to look for unique and interesting items, so they will look at these message boards frequently.

Internal Message Boards

Some employers have a message board where their employees can post things that they wish to sell. If your employer has this type of deal, try using that and selling it through the message board. Odds are that you won't have to pay for shipping fees because that employee works in the same building as you do.

Finding community methods to buy and sell are becoming increasingly popular. From using social media to buy and sell to using the message board in the downtown area, you might be surprised at the money you can get for what you wish to sell.

Chapter 7- Keeping Up to Date on Items that Sell for Big Money

Times change. Along with time, prices of items and the ways in which they are sold will also change. It's important that you keep yourself educated and up to date on pricing trends and how they affect the items that you are trying to sell. It could be either good or bad when thrift store reselling is in the picture. However, you can keep yourself from taking some major losses if you know what to look for and how to work around it.

It is amazing how an item can change in popularity in a short amount of time. Once it becomes popular, everyone wants it, and once it loses its popularity, then no one wants it. However, there are items that will never lose their worth, and that is one area that you can focus on when buying and selling.

Don't be afraid to go research prices and selling prices often. Depending on what you're looking at, you may save yourself money by refraining from buying it in the first place. The great part about technology is that you can check the prices in real time while you're standing in front of the item in question. There are apps and websites that can be accessed through a mobile device that will tell you what the item is worth before you even take it to the cash register.

Going online before you go thrift store shopping is another way to find out what is selling at that moment in time. Knowing what you're looking for and what people are buying can be valuable when faced with a huge thrift store. Who knows, a certain type of item could be more popular today than it was just a week ago! Don't be left in the dust because you didn't take the time to do the research before you started shopping.

If you go thrift store shopping regularly, then you might want to keep up on the trends via your computer and online selling sites. They are the most reliable and up to date way to know what people are buying and how much they are paying for what they're buying.

Finally, don't be left behind because you're too busy to keep up on trends. You might just run into the right item at the right time. Knowing that this item can earn you big money will make your perseverance worth it!

Good luck on finding your items and selling them for the best price possible! You can do this!

Conclusion

Thank you again for downloading this book!

I hope this book was able to help you to understand what an opportunity lies in the walls of your local thrift store. Earning money can be easy when you know what to look for and how to sell it to waiting buyers!

The next step is to do some research and find out what is popular today that you can make some big money on. Knowing that the thrift stores are a treasure chest, use them to help you gain that extra cash!

RESELLER SECRETS
TO DOMINATING A THRIFT STORE
REVEALED

40 Creative Ways To Use All Of The Sections In A Thrift Store To Make Huge Money Selling On eBay And Amazon

RICK RILEY

Introduction

I want to thank you and congratulate you for downloading the book, Reseller Secrets To Dominating A Thrift Store Revealed: 40 Creative Ways To Use All Of The Sections In A Thrift Store To Make Huge Money Selling On eBay And Amazon

This book contains proven steps and strategies on how to use all of the sections of your thrift store in creative ways so that you can make a huge profit selling on eBay and Amazon.

This book is going to teach you how you can use your creativity paired with the items you can regularly find at thrift stores to turn a huge profit. Unlike other books, this book is not just about finding those special treasures, but how you can use literally any item that you find in a thrift store to make a profit.

You will be walked through the different sections of a thrift store and given in great detail ideas that you can use to make a profit. At the end of this book you are going to be given tips ensuring that you are able to turn a profit and ensuring that you only purchase items that you will be able to resell.

Thanks again for downloading this book, I hope you enjoy it!

Chapter 1
How to Buy and Sell Clothing From a Thrift Store

Often times it can be difficult to make very much money off of clothing that you purchase at a thrift store, unless you are able to find high end clothing. Of course we know that we can flip this type of item for a profit, but what about all the other clothing you find? In this chapter we are going to go over some creative ways for you to flip thrift store clothing and make a profit from it on eBay or Amazon.

1. Many times you can find a lot of plain t-shirts at thrift stores for pennies, but most people are not looking for this type of item when they shop eBay or Amazon. You should not pass these up however. Instead think about buying all of the white, cream and grey t-shirts, dresses and pants you can find. Then, take one day out of the month and spend it tie-dying them. So many people love the tie-dye look but they either don't have time to do it themselves or they simply don't understand how it is done. You can sell these tie-dye shirts for about $5 each so spending a few hours a month tie-dying thrift store clothing can turn into big profits!

2. If you go to the thrift store on a day when they are having what is called a bag sale, you can get a lot of clothing for pennies! A bag sale is when a store will allow you to put as much as you can in a bag and they charge one flat rate, usually a dollar for the entire bag, instead of charging per piece. Of course you are going to end up with a bunch of non-brand name clothing that you will not be able to sell. So when you get home, go

through the clothing and start cutting them into small quilting squares. Once you have enough squares, you can make a simple quilt and sell it for up to $150!

3. Make your own designs by using thrift store clothing as a base. Often times you will see shirts or light sweaters at thrift stores and wonder why anyone would ever wear that. However, have you ever asked yourself what you could actually do with it? For example, you may think that no one wants to wear a striped sweater, but have you ever considered that it could be turned into a simple cardigan that people would love? Maybe add a few buttons and really make it pop. You can also advertise this merchandise as one of a kind.

4. Grab a bunch of sweaters at the end of winter when the stores are trying to clear out their winter clearance and make some sweater sleeve boot socks. Boot socks are all the rage right now and you can make $5 a pair easy if they are cute. Try to focus on sweaters that have lace around the wrist or another pretty design and you will not be able to keep these on the shelves!

5. You will also notice that when you are looking through thrift store clothing there are a ton of gorgeous jeans for girls and women but many of them may be worn in one spot or even have a tear. You can take these home and use lace to embellish these jeans making them look amazing. Again you can advertise these as one of a kind and make a huge profit. If you find jeans with holes in them, you can ask for a discount at thrift stores making your profit even larger!

6. Another thing you can do with old jeans is cut them off into shorts, add lace trim around the bottom of the shorts and sell them for $15-$20 each. You just need to make sure that the lace is not scratchy or too rough on the skin. You can usually find this type of lace at thrift stores in the arts and crafts section for a few dollars. We will get more into that later though.

7. Remember how I told you that you can find a ton of old t-shirts at thrift stores? One thing that I love to do is go to the men's section and look for the largest t-shirts I can find, add some elastic to the inside of the t-shirt where my waist is and I have a cute dress. You can get t-shirts for almost nothing at a thrift store and this is another good item to stock up on when your store has a bag sale. It only takes a few minutes to add the elastic. These dresses sell for about $20 each and if you want to get creative and add some more details, you can charge even more!

If you want to be able to make money off of anything you find in the clothing section of a thrift store then you are going to have to get creative. Most clothing items have been donated because the previous owners knew there was no real money to be made with them. Unless you are in a high end thrift store you are not going to find a ton of brand name clothing. Even then if you do go to a high end thrift store, there is not much profit to be made after you pay what they are charging. Instead, offer one of a kind creations you have made from thrift store finds!

Chapter 2
How to Make Money Buying Shoes at Thrift Stores

Another item you will find in abundance at thrift store is shoes. The problem is that these shoes are not always in the best condition and often times they are scuffed up or just look worn out. In this chapter we are going to go over creative things you can do with these old shoes so that you can sell them on eBay or Amazon for a profit.

1. This is one of my favorite things to do and it doesn't take very much time at all. I find several pair of old heels. It does not matter the color as long as the shoe is not broken down or falling apart. I do not pay attention to the way the shoe looks, only that the shoe is not flattened out or the heel is not falling off. Once I get these shoes home I will cover them with glue and then sprinkle a ton of glitter on them. This way I am creating my own glitter shoes. One thing I have learned is that it is very hard to find glitter shoes for women and for girls, so these sell very quickly if you do a good job applying the glitter!

2. Find an old pair of flats at a resale shop that are no longer in fashion, but in good condition. Then, you can add lace or other material to make them look like new again. The process of gluing lace or other material onto shoes is very simple and hard to mess up as long as you are paying attention to what you are doing. The good thing is that if you do mess up you are only out a dollar or two, and you have learned what not to do along the way.

3. Adding jewels to shoes is another great idea. Simple tennis shoes can be made to look amazing if you take a few minutes and add some jewels to the area above the toe. You can also add jewels around the rim of heels to make them look new. Be creative when you are adding jewels to shoes, but remember to not go overboard. If you are paying full price for jewels, you want to make sure you are counting that into the price of the shoe. If you can't make the price of your jewels back, you may end up going out of business very quickly.

4. If you find a lot of heels that you can purchase very cheaply, you can cover them with some painters tape, leaving the toe area uncovered and use some spray paint to spice them up. One great thing about this is often times I will find 30 or 40 of the same pair of shoes at a thrift store and I am able to make them all different, as well as unique, which causes my profits to raise.

5. You will never have a problem finding plain bland heals at a thrift store and if you can get them super cheap you can make a huge profit simply by creating a bow and adding it to the shoe. Some people like to add big bows behind the heel and others prefer them on top of the shoe. However, as long as it looks cute, you will make a profit doing this.

6. Grab a pair of white high heels and cover the back of them in pearls. You will want to ensure that you have about half an inch of space between your pearls, but this gives new life to an old heel. You can also place these around the opening of the shoe, or even just a few around the toe area. If it looks good to you someone else is going to fall in love with it and purchase it from you. Again make sure you add the price of the pearls into the overall cost of the heel so you know you are making a profit.

7. Don't forget about feathers. Ladies love feathers and you can add these to old high heeled shoes for just around a dollar. This will make the shoes look completely new, original and amazing. Then you can turn around and sell them for a huge profit.

Often times people don't want to get very creative when it comes to purchasing items at thrift stores and finding ways to make a profit from them. If it was as simple as going to a thrift shop, buying items and making a profit from them everyone would do it. Sometimes you need to think of flipping thrift store items the same way you would think about flipping a house. It may take a little work but if you can double or triple your money it is always worth it.

Chapter 3
How to Make Money With Home Décor From a Thrift Store

You can find so much home décor at thrift store, but often times it looks old and worn out. Before you use any of the tips I am going to give you in this chapter make sure that you cannot make more of a profit by selling that old home décor without doing anything to it. Many times I have picked up an item with the idea of repurposing it and have found out when I got home that it was worth much more in its current condition than if I repurposed it.

1. Picture frames are a great item for you to pick up. You need to look for frames that look old with a lot of detail.

    Don't worry about the picture inside of the frame. Simply look at the frame and if it is not chipped or broken, you can take it home. Remove the glass, as well as the picture, clean up the frame and paint it. This is one of the items you want to check the value of before painting it! People are always looking for large old picture frames. If you can find one with an old photo of a person in it, you can usually get even higher profits from it.

2. Look for old trinkets as well! Old keys, locks, or tags, anything that looks old and you can create a beautiful wind chime out of it. There are people who collect wind chimes and the more unique, the more value it has. If you simply collect these trinkets and create a one of a kind wind chime you will be making a huge profit.

3. Another item that you can find an abundance of is scrabble tiles. Many stores have bags and bags of these for a dollar each. Use these to create coasters simply by gluing them together, sell them for $8 for a set of four and watch them fly off your shelves!

4. It is difficult to find full china sets at a thrift store, but what you can find is random tea cups. These can be used to make candles in and sold for about $20 a piece. It is very simple to purchase the wax and wick to make the candle and if you glue the cup to the saucer (if you can find a matching set) you can charge even more.

5. One thing that I love to do is make a huge profit out of something that doesn't cost more than a dollar. One way to do this is to purchase plastic toys. For example a small dinosaur, drill two holes in his back and place one toothbrush in each of the holes and sell it for a toothbrush holder. Parents go crazy for this type of item, but make sure you are not drilling into a toy that you could sell as is. You have to be very careful with toys when it comes to thrift stores because often times you will find that something you think has little or no value is actually worth a lot of money.

6. Purchase an old plain lamp shade and cover it with buttons or gems. Lamp shades are very expensive, but you can find them at a thrift store for around $1-$2. Clean them up and make them look new again and you can earn a huge profit. Even adding a few jewels around the top of a plain white lamp shade will easily bring in $20.

7. Take an old vase that you find at a thrift store and cover it in pennies, trinkets, buttons or gems. Use whatever you can find the cheapest at a thrift store, but make sure it looks unique. Simply use a hot glue gun to attach these to the vase.

The more unique your item the faster it is going to sell and the more profit you are going to make on it. When it comes to being creative with your items to sell them for a profit on eBay you want to make sure they are unique, but you also want to make sure it is something that someone is actually going to want to purchase. Simply having an item that is unlike any other is not going to guarantee a profit. You need to ask yourself if you would give the item as a gift or if you would purchase the item yourself. If the answer is no chances are you will not make a profit.

Chapter 4
How to Make Money Selling Arts and Crafts Items From a Thrift Store

Most thrift stores have an arts and crafts section and this can be utilized to make a ton of money. In this chapter we are going to go over the many different ways you can make money by using the arts and crafts section in your thrift store.

One great thing about thrift stores is that you can purchase crafting supplies super cheap. You have a few options when it comes to these supplies. You can gather them and use them to create your own crafts which we will discuss plenty of ideas in this chapter. You can also create lots of these supplies and sell them quickly. If you want to make the most profit you will want to use these supplies yourself.

1. Yarn is in abundance at thrift stores and the great thing about this yarn is that it is high quality yarn. You will pay less than half of what you would normally pay for it and in your spare time while you are sitting in front of the television you can crochet a blanket and sell it for $50!

2. Hair bows for little girls are selling like crazy and these only take a few minutes to make. You can purchase the ribbon at a resale shop, spend five minutes making a bow and sell it for $5 with no problems.

3. A really great thing I like to purchase is baby dolls in the arts and craft section. These usually sell for about a quarter each and you can use the material, ribbons and such that you find in the craft section to really dress them up. Doll collectors go crazy for this stuff because it is one of a kind.

4. You can use a lot of the items you find in the arts in the crafts area to embellish other items such as shoes and sell them for even more. Remember the more you can save at a thrift store, the higher your profit will be, so that means taking advantage of all that the thrift store has to offer.

5. Use the fabric to wrap around old or cheap picture frames to make them look amazing. You can also create a peg board out of these fabric wrapped picture frames. You can also make a chalkboard out of them. Remember creativity counts here!

6. Fake flowers are something thrift stores never seem to run out of and you can use these in a variety of ways. For example, you can add a flower to your hair bows and charge a little more. You can make barrettes that are several different flowers in a short amount of time and sell them or add the flowers to head bands. You can also add these flowers to the picture frames and give them a bit of personality.

7. Use a picture frame and a few of the supplies from the arts and crafts section and create some amazing 3D art work to sell. You will find that this type of item is going to sell quickly, again because it will be unique to your store. Buyers cannot go looking for a cheaper price and this is what you want. Of course you want to have items in your store that cannot be found other places. You also want to make sure your customers can find items at your store that they can find nowhere else. So, use your imagination and start making money!

It will really depend on the different types of arts and craft supplies that your store carries, as well as the amount of work you are willing to put into a project. You do want to make sure that you are not putting more work into a project than you will be paid for. For example if it is going to take you 3 days to complete a project and the value is only going to be $30, that is not a project you should really concern yourself with.

Most of the tips in this book can be done in your spare time. It is understandable that you are not going to take your normal 40 hours each week that you normally spend on purchasing thrift store items and selling them to work on this type of thing. These items are either for your spare time or for when it is hard for you to find items to resell.

Sometimes thrift stores go through dry periods where they just don't have any treasures to be found. That is when you should start selling these items. I suggest that while you are able to find treasures at your thrift stores that you still work on a few projects in your spare time. That way if the time comes where you have found nothing to sell, you can fall back on these items and still continue to earn money.

Chapter 5
How to Buy Small Appliances at Thrift Stores and Make Money

It is a little more difficult for you to get creative with small appliances and electronics. However, I want to include this chapter because I want you to understand that you really can make money with every section in your thrift store!

1. Watch for items that sell well but are not often found at thrift stores. One example being that I can go into any local thrift store and find bread makers. I can also go on eBay, look up bread maker and find the same one listed for $13 ending in 3 hours and no one has bid on it. The same thing goes for a George Foreman grill. You can purchase these for almost nothing any day of the week from a thrift store, list them on eBay for $2 and you will not be able to sell it for much profit at all. So make sure you are looking for rare items.

2. Food processors are one of the top five small appliances selling on eBay right now. You have to be very careful when you are looking for one to flip, because you want to get a multi-purpose food processor. A normal food processor may sell at some point, but what people are looking for right now is a way to save counter space and save themselves from having to purchase two different appliances when they can find one to do the work. Watch for multi-purpose small appliances, these will bring you the highest profits.

3. Rice cookers are another one of those multi-purpose items that you can sell for a profit. Rice cookers not only cook rice but the high end rice cookers can be used

for stews, soups as well as a variety of other foods. This makes buyers willing to pay top dollar for them.

4. Anything vintage will sell as well, even small vintage appliances. You need to make sure that these have all of their cords and it is best if you can find them still in their original boxes with any books that came with them. It does not matter what the appliance is when it comes to vintage, as long as it is in good condition.

5. Meat grinders are another item that you will be able to purchase from a thrift store and make a huge profit from but you need to make sure all the pieces are included. If you have a customer who is expecting an entire meat grinder and even one piece is missing, you will end up having to refund the money and you will have one upset customer.

6. Finally you should keep your eye out for flour grinders. Many people have gotten into grinding their own flour. Some of these people have decided it was too much of a hassle and are selling or donating their grinders to thrift stores. You can pick these up for $15-$20 and sell them for a huge profit, often up to $200.

Those are all of the tips I am going to give you when it comes to selling small appliances that you find at thrift stores. One of the reasons for this is because you have to consider shipping when it comes to large heavy items and many people do not want to deal with that hassle. The other reason is that selling different small appliances is very easy, all you have to do is ensure it is a brand name, it is in good working condition, and is something that you cannot find every day at a thrift store.

When it comes to electronics the same rules apply. For smaller electronics such as CD players or Walkmans, you need to carry some batteries around with you as well as a tape and CD that you know works and a set of headphones. This way you can test the device and make sure they actually do work. Often times just because something says it works at a thrift store does not really mean it works.

Chapter 6
Other Items You Can Profit From in a Thrift Store

I want to give you a few more ideas that you can use to make a profit from thrift store items. These are items that really did not fit in the other sections of this book, but that I still feel they are very important. In the final chapter I will give you some tips that will help to ensure you make the most from your items.

1. Coffee cups are a great way to make money on eBay. These are often over looked but they can be bought cheap and sold for a huge profit. This is an item that you can purchase as is and make a huge profit. Look for Disney mugs, Smurfs or even Peanuts. The only thing you have to do to make money!

2. Another way to make a profit from coffee mugs is to grab some nail polish and a bowl of water. Put a few drops of different color nail polishes in the water and quickly dip your cup in the nail polish. Pull the cup out and you will have personally designed cups that you can sell for a profit. Plain colored coffee mugs sell for about a quarter a piece at a thrift store and you can sell them for $7-$12 each.

3. Grab those white coffee mugs and using some chalk board paint and create chalk board coffee mugs. Add a piece of chalk and you can sell these for $16-$20 each!

4. You can create your own throw pillows from the material that you purchase at a thrift shop. You can also purchase the ones that are already made, use an iron to

add a cute saying and people will go crazy over them. Remember there is always someone out there looking to purchase what you have to sell.

5. Curtains are a great way to make money from flipping thrift store items, but you will find that you will not really be able to sell the curtains you find as is. Most of the curtains you will find will be lace panels. You can take these panels and add some of the material you found at the thrift store and make beautiful unique curtains. Using this same idea you can make cute shower curtains that will sell quickly and for a huge profit!

6. Right after Christmas is a great time to stock up on Christmas decorations such as Christmas balls. You can use these items to make wreaths or other Christmas décor. If you have room to store these and are not looking for a quick turn around, you will see large profits in the following year.

7. Jewelry always sells great but right now you can sell handmade jewelry for a huge profit. There are tons of books out there telling you how to make the jewelry, but if you really want to put your thrift store finds to work, grab some books and make your own beads out of the pages of the books. It is a very simple process, and it only takes some book pages, glue and a straw. You can sell the beads on their own or make cute jewelry out of them.

8. Cell phone covers can be purchased for a few cents at thrift stores, add a few gems and you have a new unique cell phone cover. Make sure you know what type of cell phone the cover fits before listing it and don't copy someone else's creating, remember uniqueness counts in this area.

9. Cell phone chargers are another item that you can find in abundance at the thrift store and can usually get them for pennies as well. Remember you want to make them unique. I have seen jeweled cell phone chargers go for as much as $20. These are small and easy to ship and you don't have to worry about them breaking during shipment.

10. Bedding is a great item that you don't have to be creative with but often times gets over looked, especially childrens bedding. Again this will be Disney, Peanuts, The Smurfs and such. You want to look for vintage bedding that is in good condition. It is best if it comes in a complete set but simply selling the sheets without a blanket will earn you a great profit as well.

11. Use old watches that you find at thrift stores and place them on the face of a clock instead of numbers. So many people collect clocks and this one is sure to sell quickly. You don't have to worry about doing any wiring or electrical work, simply glue the watches to the face of an old clock you find at the thrift store.

12. Use old t-shirts to create a t-shirt necklace. You can create t-shirt necklaces or infinity scarfs out of any plain t-shirt and it doesn't have to be in good condition either. This is a great way to make $10 off of a bunch of t-shirts you paid 10 cents each for.

13. You can purchase Easter decorations after Easter and just like the you would do for the Christmas décor, make wreaths or other decorations out of it. Hold it until the following year and watch your profits soar. Again, this is only if you are not looking for immediate profits and have the space to store the items.

14. Stuffed animals are an item that you don't have to be very creative to sell. You have to have an open mind when it comes to looking for them in thrift stores. Watch for items such as Puff the Magic Dragon, the original Smurfs, Scooby and other 80's plush toys. Many people think that beanie babies will sell, but the truth is that you are going to make more of a profit on these simple stuffed animals than you ever will on beanie babies.

15. Cuff links are usually easy to find when you go to thrift stores and they are very cheap. You can use these to create many different kinds of jewelry including cute earrings. Not only can you make a profit on these but you can sell them very quickly.

16. Halloween costumes are a great find! If you can find small ones and turn them in to pet costumes you can sell them year round. People love to dress up their animals and pet costumes sell quickly, so if you are looking for a quick profit make sure you try this.

Chapter 7

A Few Final Tips on Selling

To finish up this book I want to give you a few extra tips to help ensure you pick up the best items and make the most profit possible.

One of the first things you need to do is make sure that when you are purchasing clothing you check them for any flaw. I discussed how you could embellish torn jeans, however you need to make sure the tear is in an area that will look good if it is embellished and that the hole is not too big.

When it comes to other pieces of clothing such as t-shirts, you want to make sure there are no flaws because you will not be able to resell it no matter how creative you are with the design.

You also need to do a smell test. If clothing has a bad, moldy or musty smell you do not want to purchase them. Sometimes you can get this smell out by washing the clothing in white vinegar, but I have found it is not worth the risk of losing money.

Know what your budget is! This is one of the most important things you can learn. Often times people get so caught up in purchasing items to resell that they forget that they need to focus on how much they are spending. I advise that if you are going to use these tips you do it with one item at a time, see how your item sells and then decide how much you are willing to invest. Always make sure you stick to that budget.

The next tip I have for you is that you should choose a niche. This means that if you want to sell glitter shoes and jeweled purses that you really need to stick to this type of item as much as possible.

Time versus money. Many of these projects are very simple, they can be done within a few minutes, but for some of them you will need to weigh the time it takes you to complete the project versus the money you are making. If the money is not worth your time, then you should not do that specific project.

Create a formula for your success. You need to have a plan. How much time you will spend in thrift stores each week, what type of items you are looking for, how much money you are willing to invest and how much time you are willing to invest in listing products.

Finally make sure that your descriptions are detailed. You don't want to make a description that is only a few words because that will not draw the buyer's attention. Make sure you give as much detail as possible.

Conclusion

Thank you again for downloading this book!

I hope this book was able to help you to find creative ways to use all the areas of your thrift shops to make the most profit.

The next step is to choose one tip from this book, try it and see how quickly your item sells. If the item sells quickly, go ahead and invest a bit more time if not then move on to the next tip that interests you the most.

Finally, if you enjoyed this book, then I'd like to ask you for a favor, would you be kind enough to leave a review for this book on Amazon? It'd be greatly appreciated!

DIY PROJECTS
Selling Creative
DIY Projects
Online

**40 EASY DIY PROJECTS THAT CAN BE DONE
QUICKLY AND SOLD ONLINE FOR HUGE PROFITS**

RICK RILEY

Introduction

I want to thank you for downloading this book, *DIY Projects: Selling Creative DIY Projects Online: 40 Easy DIY Projects That Can Be Done Quickly and Sold Online for Huge Profits.*

This book contains proven steps and strategies on how to find easy projects that are useful to others and can be sold for profits. People often like the look and feel of homemade goods, but they either lack the time or motivation to do them themselves. By making and selling homemade projects online, you can find an audience that will appreciate your work and pay you for what you do!

Do you have a knack for making things that others want in their home? Do others ask you to make them items for their home? If this is something that sounds familiar, then why not use your talent for making items that others will pay good money for? By taking the time to put together homemade projects and selling them online, you can show your flair for handiwork while making a profit. This book will tell you some of the top projects that people are spending good money on. Why not be a part of this growing trend?

Thanks again for downloading this book, I hope you enjoy it!

Chapter 1- What People are Looking for

As you may well know, most of the items that we use and look at on a daily basis are mass produced for profits. We might be lucky to find a few homemade items in craft stores or at garage sales, but for the most part, we live in a day and age where almost everything is mass produced, having no personal value to it whatsoever. Do you find that you wish to find items that are unique and special to you? Having items that not everyone can have is a desire of many people. However, in a busy world, many people don't have the time or motivation to make these things for themselves.

If you find that you love do it yourself home projects and that others appreciate your work, it might be time to put your skills to work for your pocketbook. There are hundreds of do it yourself projects out there that people like but don't have the time to do. By taking these projects and making them yourself, you can actually sell these to those who cannot do it for themselves. Do you have the time and the motivation to provide these to those who cannot make them for themselves?

There is a wide variety of items out there that people like and wish that they could make for themselves. If you have gone on social media lately, you have seen do it yourself hacks posted to your friends' pages that they really like. The fact is, they might like the idea, but they will never actually make the item for themselves. You can also find a whole array of do it yourself projects by simply going on sites such and Pinterest. People are constantly sharing ideas that others really like.

You might have a creative ability to see the beautiful in the ordinary. If you can picture ways that you can make your life better or easier by making your own items, then you are on the right track for being able to make great items that you can sell to others. Others will enjoy your work and pay good money for something that may have just popped into your head at a moment's notice. Don't discount your small ideas because they can yield large results!

So, whether you excel at making homemade clothing or accessories, or small pieces of unique furniture, take your skills to the next level and let those who like them purchase them from you. You never know, it could end up being a winning business venture. If your imagination is already thinking up all the possibilities, and you have time and motivation to make it happen, then let's take a look at how you can make your own do it yourself projects a business!

Take a moment and think about what you can do at home that others may want in their homes. In the following chapters, we will look at some quick do it yourself ideas that can be valuable to you.

Chapter 2- Easy Decorative Pieces

When people decorate their homes or offices, they often look for unique pieces that they can display. No one likes to have someone come into their home and exclaim that they saw that at the local retail store. Having unique and handmade items are a must for people like this. What can you make to cater to this crowd?

Taking a look at the most popular do it yourself websites, I have come up with some ideas that will be easy and useful for any crowd. No matter what your skill level, do it yourself projects will turn out unique. It might take a few tries to get them just right, but you won't know unless you try them!

Wood Crate Furniture

Wooden crates can be bought at a relatively inexpensive price and a lot of things can be done with it. You can take a spin on the crate itself. Try using paints and other decorations to make these crates into shelves or tables that will be unique to the home. These crates can be nailed together and made to be in the shape of whatever item of furniture that you wish to make.

Pallet Makeovers

Old shipping pallets can be painted and converted into a number of do it yourself items. You can make an herb garden, a craft organization system, or even furniture from these old pallets. The great part is, retailers will often just throw old pallets out, so you can come by them for next to nothing and make a huge profit from whatever you choose to make with them.

Decorative Vases

You can buy glass containers at craft stores. Try wrapping them with rubber bands and spray painting the outside of the container with frosted spray paint. After the paint has dried, take the rubber bands off, and you will have a frosted glass vase with a unique design on the sides! You can find several things that can go against the glass to make different designs. Lace is another material that will give your vases a beautiful and unique finish.

Window Treatments

You can create beautiful and unique curtains and valances by using fabric and other materials. There are many patterns out there for window treatments that don't need you to sew anything. All you would basically need is a yard of fabric and some string to make a beautiful and unique window covering. You can design several types of these to catch a buyer's attention.

Personalized Photo Frames

Places that sell photo frames will often sell old or damaged pieces for much less than full price. You can take advantage of this and buy these frames and create new frames. Spray paint, stencils and hot glue can be used to apply new designs and colors to an otherwise bland frame. I have seen ones made that have silk flowers glued to the corners. These are fun and unique.

Doors into Headboards

You can repurpose old doors that you find in thrift stores and turn them into headboards. These aren't just any headboards, but these are decorative headboards. This will take some fabric, insulation, and a staple gun, but you can create a headboard by applying fabric to an old door. The insulation will give the headboard a padded feel. You can also paint an old door with different designs to make a decorative headboard that will catch people's attention.

Having unique décor that you can sell will draw people to you. Many do it yourself decorations and furniture items can use old pieces of furniture and repurposing it to make something new and unique. Try looking around at a thrift store and putting a new spin on some of the items that you see lurking in the aisles. Your creative touch could be what someone was looking for!

Chapter 3- Soaps and Candles

There is a personal touch to having a handmade soap or candle. Anyone can go to the store and purchase soap and candles, but ones that are personal and just right usually come from someone's hands. Surprisingly enough, soaps and candles can easily be made and personalized just the way you want them to be. It takes just a few ingredients, but you can add your own colors and scents to them, making them something unique.

Candles and soaps make wonderful gifts for birthdays, weddings, and holidays. Since store bought candles and soaps really don't have a personal touch, making your own and packaging them in a crafty and creative way can help you to sell many of them. By finding just the right product and the right packaging, your DIY candles and soaps can be hit for purchasing for gifts!

Personally, I love to make my own candles. It only takes a few minutes to melt down my wax and add the scent that I want it to be. I can also put these candles in any container that I want to, so I'm not limiting the candle to a simple glass jar. How would you make a candle or a soap unique? Let's take a look at some ideas for homemade soaps and candles!

Mason Jar Candles

Putting a candle in a mason jar can be a simple, but classic statement. Mason jars typically signify antique or classic, so having these candles will give you that type of a feel. After melting down and scenting your wax, pour it into mason jars.

Take a wick and put it in the middle, using a toothpick to hold it up at the top until the wax cools. Once the wax cools, you have a simple and classic looking candle!

Bottle Cap Candles

Old fashioned bottle caps can be remade into candles that give you a nostalgic feel. Find the old metal bottle caps, clean them out, and pour your wax in them. Put a wick in the center and wait for them to cool. These can be a fragrant and decorative expression in your home.

Peppermint Soap

In order to make soaps, you will need to buy a good soap base to work with. These can often be found in craft stores. Starting with a soap base, you add the necessary ingredients and essential oils to give it its scent. For peppermint soap, you use a soap base and peppermint essential oil to make a lovely smelling soap. You can add color with soap colorant and pour them into the molds of your choice. These are typically ready within ten minutes!

Lavender Soap

Lavender soap is made much like the peppermint soap, except you use lavender essential oil in order to give the soap base its fragrance. You can also give this soap a purple coloring by using soap colorant. There are many types of molds out there, so you can be creative and use molds that are unique and will gain peoples' attention.

Pringle Can Pillar Candles

If you're looking to make a pillar candle from scratch, melt down your wax, add the colors and scents, and put it into a Pringle chip can. Take a wick and place it in the center, held up with a stick at the top. Once the wax dries, you simple cut the can off of the candle, and you have a pillar candle without having to buy expensive molds!

Heat Transferred Designs

A fun way to make personalized candles is to draw or write on wax paper with permanent markers. After you have a design that you like, wrap it around a pillar candle and secure the wax paper with tape. Take a blow dryer and heat the image until it transfers onto the candle. Slowly remove the remaining wax paper, and you will have a beautiful and decorative candle! Just think of how many possible designs you can put onto a candle!

Olive Oil Candles

Try putting olive oil into mason jars. Take essential oils and put into the olive oil and place a wick in the middle. This will give you a quick and easy liquid candle that can also be stylish and decorative! You can also try to add coloring to the oil to make the candles various colors!

Sand Jar Candles

If your home has a beach feel to it, then sand jar candles will be a great accent. Take a Mason jar and place sand in the bottom. Take a stick candle and place it in the center of the sand, gluing it to the bottom of the jar. Place sea shells and other decorations that will give the candle a beach feel.

Homemade Hand Soap

Homemade hand soap can be made by using oils and ingredients in your home. Using a soap base, you can add ingredients such as coconut oil, shea butter, olive oil, and honey to make your own soaps at home. These too can have essential oils added to them in order to give them scents. Mixing in ingredients that will treat certain types of skin will give them a personal treating element while giving you the scent that you enjoy.

People love to buy homemade candles and soaps for gifts. You will see that these will be great sellers around the holidays. Making a nice array of either candles or soaps, or even both, can be a huge seller. People like creativity and variety, so give them a little bit of both!

Chapter 4- Furniture Refurbishing

Nowadays, there are a lot of people who enjoy having unique and creative furniture. There are many do it yourself ideas for making furniture into something beautiful and creative. The great thing is that people don't have the time or motivation to make these unique pieces. There are tons of ideas for how you can use bookshelves and other pieces of furniture to create beautiful and unique pieces.

Do you have a knack for refinishing furniture in ways that would complement someone's home? If you can find furniture in thrift stores or at garage sales that you turn into something fantastic, then you can make these projects a nice money maker. Here are some ideas for ways that you can refurbish furniture to resell for a profit.

Building Furniture

The thought of building furniture can seem overwhelming, but there are some simple and elegant pieces that can be built using just a few materials. For example, you can build a simple frame and place storage bins in it to create a set of drawers. Old pallets used for shipping can be made into spice racks or herb gardens by adding wood in just the right places. Building your own furniture doesn't have to be hard. As long as it is unique, it will catch someone's attention!

Refinishing Worn Out Pieces

Sometimes the old pieces of furniture that you find at garage sales and thrift stores simply need to be refinished in order to show the original beauty of the piece. This can take some time and effort, but if you find a good piece of furniture that can really show its beauty, you can make some good money after refinishing and selling it. Take the furniture and sand off the old finish. Then apply a new finish to make the natural elements of the wood stand out. It might take a few coats of finish, but you can revive a beautiful piece of furniture with a little TLC.

Painting and Decorating Furniture Pieces

There are numerous do it yourself projects that have you paint the furniture. This can be a white color or any other color that would be unique and bring out the beauty of the furniture. You may also have to replace knobs and handles on the furniture in order to make the overall effect something to be admired.

Reupholster Old Furniture

Sometimes you can find furniture that has fabric that is worn. You can actually remove the fabric from these pieces and replace it with new and fresh upholstery. Good examples of projects that would be easy and work well for reselling would be easy chairs or dining room chairs. These have very little upholstery, so you will have to put little effort into replacing it. There might also be wood on these chairs, so think about a good combination of finish and upholstery when you take on the project. The finished product can be beautiful.

Add Decorative Accents to Enhance Furniture

After repainting or refinishing a piece of furniture, you can go a step further and add enhancements to it that will add even more character to the piece. For example, you can add stenciling or painting to the piece can add a whole new dimension to the piece that cannot be store bought. Don't be afraid to have a vision for the piece of furniture that is before you. People want to find unique pieces of furniture and what you have created might just be what they have been seeking!

Repurposing Furniture

Sometimes, old furniture will outlive its usefulness for what it was originally intended for. A part may be broken and unable to be repaired, or you might find that it could serve a better use if it is converted into a new type of furniture. There are numerous ideas for furniture that can be repurposed and used for new and different things than what it was originally built for. Some of the best pieces of furniture are ones that have been converted from another piece of furniture. One of the best examples of repurposing that I have seen includes taking wooded crates and nailing them together to create items such as shelves and coffee tables. The wooden crates may not be useful to you in their original form, but as a piece of furniture, such as a table, they show a greater potential. Use your imagination when you look at furniture. You might just come up with something that no one else has!

Do it yourself furniture has become increasingly popular. People love to have unique furniture in their homes, so providing a way for them to do that will guarantee you the ability to sell your do it yourself projects to them. You need to have a creative imagination in order to breathe new life into furniture that seems to have no life left in it. Try taking a look at other do it yourself furniture projects that are circulating on the internet to give yourself some ideas as to what you can do to make creative and unique furniture that you can sell for a good amount of money.

Chapter 5- Apparel, Jewelry, and Accessories

If you think that handmade apparel is for old ladies, think again! There has been a huge boost in popularity in the younger crowd for handmade apparel and accessories. There are many different ways to go about making these items, but the uniqueness of each individual piece will help you to make them shine when trying to sell them.

Do you have the talent to quilt, knit or crochet? These are all crafts that can produce items that can be worn. You can even buy premade garments and spruce them up in a unique way.

If you're rearing to figure out what you can make that will sell,

let's take a look at some handmade apparel, accessories and jewelry that you can sell for money!

Crocheted and Knitted Hats and Scarves

People love the unique touch that knitting and crochet can add to hats and scarves. Even if you're not catering to the winter weather, there are types of hats and scarves that are popular year round. Fashion scarves can be worn in any season, and hats can be made for cold or warm weather. If you knit or crochet, find some patterns and make some of these accessories. Try putting a spin on the pattern to make them unique. People will love the handmade and unique quality of crocheted and knitted items.

Sweaters, Jackets, and Cover-ups

Crochet and knitting can also be used to make gorgeous sweaters, jackets and swimsuit cover-ups. You can make the looks different by using different types of yarn and different colors. Depending on the type of garment you are making, you will want to be careful what material is used. I have seen patterns for the most beautiful sweaters and jackets that will be a great addition to a professional's wardrobe.

String Bracelets

A new trend in fashion has girls wearing bracelets that are made of colored string and yarn. These bracelets can either be crocheted or braided, and beads and other accessories can be added to them as they are being crafted. Try making some unique designs in these types of bracelets. You can even go beyond the bracelets and make choker necklaces. Create your own styles and sell them to those who are looking for a unique take on fashion!

Fabric Handbags

Fabric or quilted handbags are extremely popular. However, you will find that the makers of these unique bags charge outrageous prices for them. Try going to a fabric store and picking up your own fabrics and making your own handbags. You can sell them at a fraction of the cost of what the retailers sell them for, and you may even be able to customize them for people looking for something unique.

Crocheted or Knitted Handbags

There are many different designs of handbags that can be knitted or crocheted and will add a unique twist to any wardrobe. You can make these in a variety of colors and designs. Depending on the weight of the yarn you choose, you can make a multitude of different designs that will suit any taste. Use your imagination. You can cater to different age groups by the colors and styles you choose, making handbags a very versatile item to play with!

Headbands and Hair Accessories

Fabric headbands have grown in popularity recently. These can either be crafted from fabric or made by knitting and crochet. Creating a unique headband will draw attention to your craft, and girls will love that their head accessories do not look like anyone else's. With the knitted and crocheted variety, you can do the same bead and decorative work that you would use for the bracelets. Use your imagination! Also, you can use yarn to crochet add-ons for bobby pins and other hair clips. Using hot glue and other decorations can also add a unique touch to any hair accessory.

Leg Warmers

Leg warmers and boot cuffs are a popular fashion statement among the young women. These add a pop of color to the area between the top of the boot and the pants. You can make these by working a simple round pattern with either knitting or crocheting. Depending on the material that you use, you can really make an endless number of varieties of this popular accent.

Handmade garments and accessories are consistently increasing in popularity, making them a good choice to make and sell to the public. By seeing what types of clothing and accessories are popular, you can easily make your own at a fraction of the cost and sell them for less than what someone would pay for them at a retail establishment. Don't be afraid to be creative. Let your hands do the talking and let your imagination take your creations to places you would never have thought imaginable. People will appreciate your creativity!

Chapter 6- Where to Sell Your Do it Yourself Items

Now that you have a good idea of what you can make in the way of do it yourself items, you are wondering where you can actually sell your creations for cold hard cash. There are many creative ways that you can market your goods, but not all of them will work out the way that you hope for them to. So, we are going to take a look at some ways you can get your handmade goods out there and get the money that you want from them. Also, I'm going to give you some ideas on how to price your items to sell. By understanding how to market and price your items, you will be ready to make your do it yourself goods into money!

Online Websites

You can pretty much reach anyone online. The world has gone online, and that is one of the key arenas where you can market and sell items with little to no effort. The most that selling online requires is a product and a good website. So, with that said, let's look at some of the websites where do it yourself items can be sold easily and quickly.

The first site is Etsy. This website offers anything handmade. So, since most of your DIY items are handmade, this is one of the best places you can begin. For Etsy, you set up a "shop" where you list your items and post pictures of them. You will also have an asking price for each item. People can go through and search your shop and buy whatever you have listed. Once your item has sold, you will pay a listing fee for the site and ship the item. Whatever you have left is what you made from the item. Etsy is easy to use and attracts millions of people on a daily basis.

Another good website to sell the larger items on would be Craigslist. While you might be hesitant to list on this site, there are a lot of honest people out there who will give you money for you item. You need to have good pictures of your item and a complete description. When selling it, make sure that you are getting cash only for it and that you meet your buyer in a public location. Furniture and other large items might sell better here.

As always, eBay is an excellent website for selling just about anything. Just like Etsy, you will post a picture and description of your item and let the public view it. However, with eBay, you can choose to auction off the item or sell it at a fixed price. eBay may not be the first site to go to for selling handmade items, but if you feel that it will sell here, give it a try!

Craft Fairs

Every summer, you will see tons of craft fairs in your area. Why not make some money off of it? Almost anyone can rent a booth at a craft fair, and there is such a diverse array of items that can be sold at these events that almost anything handmade will go. If you have a lot to sell and believe that you can sell it in this atmosphere, give it a try! These events will often benefit good causes, so either way, your booth rental money won't be wasted.

Sell from Home

You can sell your craft items from your home as well. Some people who are known for their DIY items can sell them from their garages and their homes. You may have to earn a reputation for your product first, but once you have a good customer base, then you will be able to market and sell out of your home without having to worry about paying fees.

Pricing to Sell

When you get ready to sell your items, it's important that you price your items in such a way that you will be able to sell them without taking a loss to your profits. So, think about how much you actually spent on the materials to make your item, the time spent making them, and how much it will take you to sell it. With all of these factors in line, find a competitive price that will allow you to have a profit without overpricing the item itself. You don't want to take a loss by pricing it too low, but you also don't want to overprice it so that it won't sell. Remember, it's homemade and you cannot price it like its brand name and new.

Making a Profit

Ultimately, you want to see a gain from your product. So, figuring out how much you sell your item for that will show a good profit is important. You want to see a return for your time and efforts, after all. Take a look at the store version of what you're selling and make your price competitive to that. You will have an edge because your item is unique, so take that into account when pricing as well.

Knowing Your Buyer

Having a buyer for your product is extremely important. Know what people are looking for, and make your items cater to them. Offer a variety of items that you know that will sell and take suggestions for new variations. By giving the public what they want, you will make the money you desire. Take all of these ideas into account when you decide to make new projects in the future.

Selling your DIY items is a great way to earn extra income. You probably will enjoy what you're selling enough to want to make more for others. It might take some experimentation at first to get the patterns and the formulas right, but once you have a good product, be ready to sell!

Chapter 7- Finding Items to Make that Will Sell

This book just covers the surface of what you can make that will sell for a profit. There are new and intriguing ideas that come out on a daily basis. To keep up with these trends, you can browse websites such as Etsy and go to DIY websites that give people ideas that will inspire them to make items for themselves. If these ideas appeal to you and you know that you can sell them, give it a try! You don't know what will sell unless you make the effort.

As you go along, you will notice that unique takes on home goods and apparel are amongst the most popular DIY projects out there. People like to make their homes and themselves more unique. If you have a talent for sewing or crafting, then you have an edge in this arena. You can find patterns and recipes that you can make changes to that will give you a wonderful and unique twist. Be as creative as you can without going overboard, though!

If you have ideas in your head that are begging to get out, give them a try. Be creative and be unique. The items that sell the most are the ones that stand out and cannot be found anywhere else. Even if you feel foolish, it really doesn't hurt to give it a try.

Another great place to find good ideas for new projects will be social media. Your friends are always sharing things that they think are cool and unique. Keep up with what they are liking and sharing and see if you can make your own renditions of them for your own profit. Also, if you search the internet, you will find that there are hundreds of websites that focus on do it yourself items. People are proud of their work and want to show it off. If you can duplicate some of the ideas efficiently, you will have a great item that you can sell and make money off of. You may not even realize that some things really can be made! Let your friends guide you and give you some ideas.

Finally, you can get some great DIY ideas by walking through thrift stores and looking at furniture and furnishings that can be redone with a unique twist. Let your imagination take root and let the voices of the thrift items speak to you. You never know, you might just have a great idea that can earn you some nice cash!

Wherever you find your ideas, keep going back to them. Even if you find yourself mass producing ski hats, you might get a better idea for something new that you can create and sell. Don't limit yourself. Allow the possibilities to flow! You will be happy that you did.

As you are on your way to making DIY items that can be sold for cash, make something for your own home as well. You can make your home a showpiece that people will see and say that they want what you have. This will give you some more ideas on what you can make that will sell for good money.

I want to wish you good luck on your venture to find DIY projects that will sell for good money. This book only covers the surface of what is out there that you can use to sell for a profit. There are numerous other ideas that I haven't even thought of that could be the next big thing. Keep your eyes and ears open and find what can make you a huge profit!

Conclusion

Thank you again for downloading this book!

I hope this book was able to help you to find some ideas for items that you can make at home and sell for a great profit. Many people look for a handmade and unique touch on many of their household items and apparel, but many either don't have the time or the creativity to make them for themselves. By doing it for them, you can earn some nice money!

The next step is to find some ideas and projects that you can make and sell. Look at different thoughts and ideas, and think of how you can package and sell them for a profit!

Finally, if you enjoyed this book, then I'd like to ask you for a favor, would you be kind enough to leave a review for this book on Amazon? It'd be greatly appreciated!